TACKLING MEN'S HEALTH

A PRACTICAL GUIDE TO HEALTH & FITNESS FOR MEN

DR. JOHN O'RIORDAN

The Tackling Series of Practical Books

Published 1992
by
On Stream
Publications Ltd
Cloghroe,
Blarney, Co.Cork.
Ireland. Tel/Fax
353 21 385798

ISBN:
1 89768597 1

Cover design: Kevin Sanquest
Printing: Litho Press

All rights reserved. No part of this publication may be copied, reproduced or transmitted in any form or by any means, without the prior permission in writing of the publishers.

Contents

Chapter 1: Lifestyle 7
How small adjustments in our daily lives can improve our health

Chapter 2: Stress 29
What it is, how to recognise it, how to deal with it

Chapter 3: Heart disease 35
Risk factors and prevention

Chapter 4: Cancer 43
Prevention, recognising skin cancer

Chapter 5: Well Man advice 47
Guide to male sex organs, problems and treatment

Chapter 6: Male infertility 67
Causes and treatment

Chapter 7: Male sexual problems 73
Difficulties with sexual activity and treatment options

Chapter 8: Contraception..85
Options for men, including vasectomy, brief guide to alternatives for women

Chapter 9: Sexually transmitted disease.......................................99
Prevention, recognition and treatment

Chapter 10: Work related disease and injury..............................109
Commonest problems, dermatitis, back pain

Chapter 11: Sports injuries...117
Understanding causes, prevention and general treatment

The author:
Dr. John O'Riordan is a general medical practitioner living in Cork. He has broadcast his advice regularly on radio and is medical advisor to numerous sports teams and organisations.

Chapter 1: LIFESTYLE

This century has seen a huge increase in the average length of life in the developed world. This has been as much due to an improvement in living conditions, with less overcrowding and better hygiene, as to medical advances, such as antibiotics.

As the average age at which we die increases, our attention is drawn to those diseases that prevent us from living to and beyond that average age.

Excluding accidents, the two most common causes of premature death in men are heart disease and cancer. What is more, when we study these, we find that alteration in our lifestyles can prevent or reduce the incidence of these diseases.

The alteration in lifestyle necessary for prevention of disease has the added benefit of improving our physical and mental well being; not alone will we live longer but our quality of life and enjoyment of it will improve.

Young men, in particular, often say 'There is no point in living longer, I'll just be senile longer.' This is untrue. The average length of life, after the onset of senility, is the same, whether it comes on at 50 years of age or 70. However, a healthy lifestyle delays the onset of senility.

FACTORS INFLUENCING HEALTH:

1. WEIGHT
2. EXERCISE
3. DIET
4. SMOKING
5. ALCOHOL
6. STRESS (SEE CHAPTER 2)

1. WEIGHT.

Not all overweight men eat more than the average. However, they do eat more than they need.

There are psychological effects from being overweight as well as increasing the risk of serious disease. The pressure to conform to the modern image of a slim shape creates difficulties for those who are overweight. This may lead to poor self-image, which may effect the person's whole outlook on life. In extreme cases this may lead to deep psychological problems, such as Anorexia Nervosa or Bulimia [Eating disorders].

DOES THE TENDENCY TO BE OVERWEIGHT RUN IN FAMILIES?

The tendency to be overweight may run in families. This may be the result of either bad dietary habits started in childhood or the effect of an inborn characteristic which makes energy burn off slower.

In most families, it is dietary habits which are responsible.

COULD I HAVE GAINED WEIGHT DUE TO MY CHANGE OF JOB?

Yes, there may be a reduction in the amount of physical work involved, as in a change from active physical work to a supervisory or sedentary job. A new job may bring on additional stress. Some respond to this stress by over-eating.

IS IT ALL ABOUT CALORIES?

Calories are a measure of energy. We put on weight if our calorie in-take exceeds the number of calories we use up. The calorie in-take alone is not the only factor in obesity. The type of food we eat has an effect independent of its calorie value. For instance, eating an apple is less likely to put on weight than eating the same apple stewed without sugar. The more difficult it is for the body to break down the food, the less likely you will gain weight from that food. Eating non processed food is therefore less likely to cause weight gain.

DOES IT MATTER WHERE I PUT ON WEIGHT?

The distribution of our excess weight also seems to be important. The common way in which excess weight is distributed in men is around the midriff, creating an apple shape. Unfortunately this distribution is associated with an increased risk of heart disease. The other way in which fat is distributed is in the buttocks or thighs, the pear shape.

There is a quick way which is useful to determine whether you are prone to heart disease:

Waist/hip ratio:

Measure your waist while in a relaxed standing position. This should be done at the level of your navel. Now measure your hips around the widest part of your buttock. Calculate the ratio by dividing your waist measurement by your hip measurement. If the result is over 1.0 you are more prone to heart disease.

Example:

    Waist = 38"
    Hip = 34"
    Waist/Hip ratio = 1.1

WHAT CONDITIONS ARE ASSOCIATED WITH BEING OVERWEIGHT?

1. DIABETES MELLITUS
2. HIGH BLOOD PRESSURE [HYPERTENSION]
3. HIGH CHOLESTEROL

Tackling Men's Health

4. STROKES - AS A RESULT OF 1/2/3 ABOVE
5. HEART DISEASE
6. VARICOSE VEINS
7. ARTHRITIS
8. HIATUS HERNIA
9. BACK INJURY
10. GALLSTONES

Weigh yourself and consult the chart below to see where you fit. The health risk increases dramatically as you go to the right of the chart.

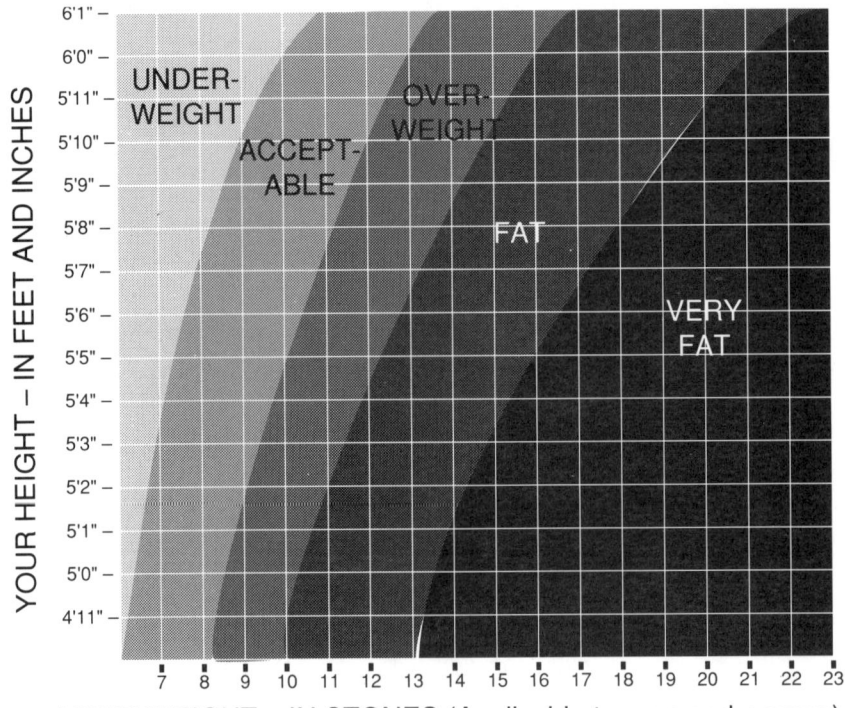

Tackling Men's Health

AM I OVERWEIGHT?

The simplest way to measure this is by seeing if you can 'pinch more than an inch'. This is done by catching the skin above the navel (belly button). The amount of fat varies in other areas of the body so the best place is here. You should be standing with your abdominal muscles relaxed. If you can pinch more than an inch you may be overweight.

The most accurate way of assessing your risk associated with being overweight is the Body Mass Index. This is measured by dividing your height in metres multiplied by that height in metres (height squared) into your weight in kilogrammes.

$$\frac{\text{WEIGHT IN KILOGRAMMES}}{[\text{HEIGHT IN METRES}]^2}$$

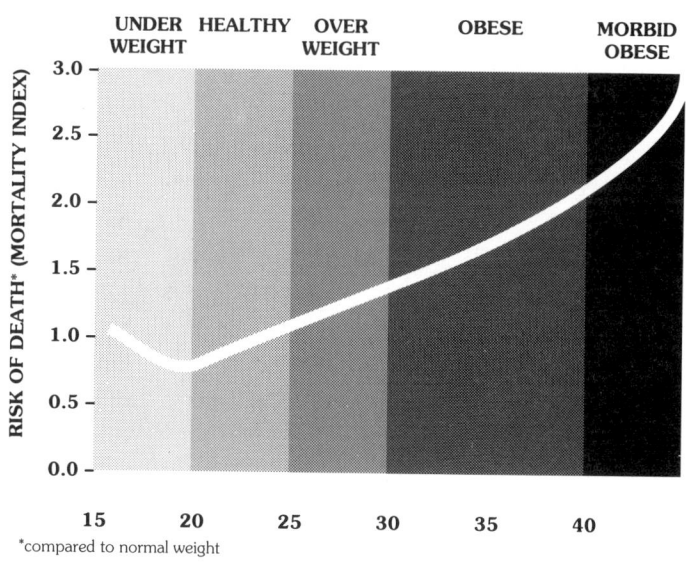

*compared to normal weight

BODY MASS INDEX (BMI)

HOW DO I CONTROL MY WEIGHT?

1. WATCH YOUR WEIGHT
2. AVOID CRASH DIETS
3. GO ON A GRADUAL WEIGHT REDUCTION DIET
4. EXERCISE MORE
5. REDUCE ALCOHOL

1. Watch your weight

    Most weight gain takes place over a long period of time and is usually due to a minor imbalance in the energy you take in [food] and the energy you use up. Energy is measured in calories.

2. Avoid crash diets

    Crash diets don't work. In fact they are counter-productive. If you go on a crash diet your body does start breaking down fat, but it also slows down the speed at which energy is used by the body. This means that when you return to a 'normal' diet your body doesn't use many calories due to this slow-down, and you put on weight with more ease than before you dieted.

3. Weight reduction diet - before you start:-

    a) Have a realistic idea of what you want to lose. The most common reason for diets failing is expecting to lose weight too quickly. To lose one or two pounds a week it is necessary to decrease your intake of calories by 750 calories a day. To put this in perspective, that would be a reduction of approximately a third of your calorie intake.

b) Allow yourself two occasions during the week when you can 'escape' from the diet. Pick a particular time for one of these escapes, such as Friday evening when you need a treat after the week's work. Keep the other escape for when you really need it.

c) Make a list of the reasons you want to lose weight. Read this list when the diet becomes difficult.

d) Get a friend to join you or just to support you while dieting.

Once you start, try to eat a wide variety of foods to avoid boredom with the diet. Eat slowly and eat regularly.

The types of foods to be avoided are listed later.

4. Exercise

Increasing your exercise increases the amount of energy you burn up.

5. Alcohol

Not only can alcoholic drinks be high in calories, (pint of beer 200-300 calories), but alcohol itself also slows down the body, and therefore reduces the amount of calories used up.

WHAT TO EAT

1. **VEGETABLES**

   unlimited amounts of most vegetables; moderate amounts of beans and lentils

2. **FRUIT**

   plenty of fresh fruit; tinned fruit in fruit juice with no added sugar; no tinned fruit in syrup; no dried fruits (raisins etc.).

3. **MEAT**

   buy smaller portions of lean meat and remove any obvious fat. Eat less meat overall.
   Within the quantity of meat include:
   More poultry, excluding duck and goose
   More offal (kidney liver)
   Moderate lean red meat
   Do not eat bacon, sausages, patés, salamis or any processed meats which include fat.

4. **FISH**

   moderate amounts
   Avoid oily fish like mackerel and canned tuna in oil. Eat more non-oily fish - cod, plaice, haddock, tuna in brine etc

5. **DAIRY PRODUCTS**

   avoid butter, cream, ice cream, full fat milk, full fat cheese. Eat eggs occasionally - two per week maximum. Use moderate amounts of reduced fat milk, yoghurt, cottage cheese, reduced fat cheese

6. **OTHERS**

   AVOID:

   Sugar, honey
   Sweets, cakes, pastries, chocolate, jam,

Sweetened drinks.
Fried foods
Flour-thickened foods - gravies, sauces, packet soups.
Sweetened cereals.

EAT:

Moderate amounts of rice, pasta.
Bread - wholemeal
Unsweetened cereals
Large amount of bran

The amount of food you need depends on your occupation and leisure activities. Giving a standard weight reduction diet to a labouring man is therefore not advisable. So, if you are trying to lose weight it is a good idea to consult a dietician, GP or a reputable organisation like WeightWatchers. Unfortunately, we often look for quick answers to the problem of overweight, and end up with bad advice from companies whose products, while attractive, are not based on scientific research and whose aim is for them to increase their profits rather than decrease our weight.

2. EXERCISE

Exercise exerts a positive effect on both our physical and mental well being.
Physical effects: The incidence of heart disease is halved by regular vigorous activity and benefits are obvious on the lungs, arteries, joints and muscles.
Mental effects: Improvement of our general well-being, improvement in sleep pattern, improvement in self image and even relief of mild depression. Exercise and the heart are discussed later in the chapter.

HOW MUCH EXERCISE DO I NEED FOR IT TO BE OF BENEFIT?

For exercise to be of benefit it should be:
Regular - 3 times a week at least
Vigorous - sufficient to cause shortness of breath and increase pulse rate to 100+
Should last at least 20 minutes

HOW SHOULD I START TO EXERCISE?

If there has been a prolonged period of inactivity - months or years - care should be taken before starting to exercise.

In an experiment, 20 days of bed rest in healthy subjects was found to have reduced the body's ability to carry oxygen by on average 30%.

IF I HAVE NOT BEEN ACTIVE WHAT SHOULD I DO

Try to establish a regular pattern to your exercise routine by exercising **at the same time of the day.**

Start gradually. You don't have to achieve 20 minutes of active exercise the first time

Allow 2-3 days between exercise at the start. Initially muscles will get tired easily and be sore the next day. Give them time to recover.

Get proper shoes and clothes. Starting to road run in a pair of old tennis shoes is folly. If you are serious, get the correct footwear designed for your chosen sport.

Do warm-up exercises before starting and warm-down exercises when finished. See sports injury chapter.

DO I NEED TO SEE MY DOCTOR BEFORE STARTING?

You need to see your doctor before starting to exercise if you:

Are over 40 years old.

Smoke over 20 cigarettes a day.

Suffer from heart disease.

Are overweight.

Have a history of exercise-induced wheeze/ asthma.

Just because you come under one of these headings does not mean you should not exercise, but merely that close supervision may be necessary in the early stages.

In particular, those with heart disease need to be closely monitored.

Do not train or play games if suffering from an infection. Fever is an absolute contra-indication to sporting activity.

Viral infections of the upper airway, like 'flu, are often associated with inflammation of the heart muscle (myocarditis). Exercise can worsen, or even cause, this inflammation. Every year there are deaths from myocarditis, most of which are preventable.

HOW HARD SHOULD I EXERCISE?

You should exercise hard enough to increase your pulse rate, within certain limits. To find these limits take your pulse and calculate them for yourself.

Take your pulse at your wrist while resting. With your palm up, put your index and

middle fingers over the outer part of the palm side of the wrist joint and count the beats for one minute. This is your resting pulse. Add that to your age and subtract the result from 220.
[Example; resting pulse 75 + age 45 =120
            220-120=100 this is the pulse range]

To calculate the effective and safe range for your pulse rate, two further calculations must be done.

(pulse range x 0.6)   +   resting pulse

(pulse range x 0.8)   +   resting pulse

The first of these results is the pulse rate we should achieve to get maximum benefit for our hearts.
The second is the upper limit to which we should allow our heart/pulse rate to get while exercising.

Take your pulse on finishing your exercise and see if you are within those limits.

3: DIET

The over availability of food in the developed world has led to problems of obesity, increased incidence of heart disease, and increased incidence of diabetes. It is not simply the availability of food but also the types of food that we are eating that is responsible for a lot of our ill-health. The processing of food has led to:

>REDUCTION IN DIETARY FIBRE.
>ADDITION OF REFINED SUGARS TO THE DIET.
>EXCESS FAT CONSUMED IN THE AVERAGE DIET.

WHAT IS FIBRE?

Fibre is the building block of plants. When we eat plants such as fruit, vegetables, cereals or lentils, we cannot break down these building blocks fully. They remain in the intestine after we have digested the food. This provides bulk without which the bowel cannot empty efficiently. A high-fibre diet is associated with a reduced incidence of:-

Constipation
Appendicitis
Diverticular Disease
Cancer of the bowel
High Cholesterol

As a high fibre diet makes us feel fuller, it can also be useful when trying to lose weight. By making us eat less refined foods, it may also be useful in the prevention of diabetes.

WHAT FOODS CONTAIN FIBRE?

1. Fruit and vegetables
2. Beans and lentils
3. Wholemeal bread, wholemeal rice, wholemeal pasta
4. Unrefined cereals, including bran

The advantages of wholemeal pastas and rice are that they are unrefined, and that the sugars they contain are 'complicated' sugars. These complicated sugars are broken down gradually by the body and so provide the body with energy over a period of time. The simple or refined sugars cause very high levels followed by sudden falls in blood sugar.

4: SMOKING.

When young people who smoke say that they see no point in giving up smoking as they are going to 'die of something anyway', they should be taken on a guided tour of a hospital. There they will see people still living with the effects of their smoking. From the lung problem wards, where they will see people on oxygen machines, to the heart problem ward, where they will see people unable to walk because of chest pain, to the ear, nose and throat wards, where they will see people unable to speak because of throat cancer, to the surgical ward where they will see people with their legs amputated. All of these problems, and more, are closely related to smoking. So, they should not just think of smoking as a killer, but as a destroyer of the quality of life. Not alone are they destroying their own lives, but also those around them are at greater risk of disease from passive smoking.

WHAT ARE THE ADVERSE EFFECTS OF SMOKING ON GENERAL HEALTH?

REDUCED EXERCISE TOLERANCE.
REDUCED RESISTANCE TO INFECTION.
NUTRITION IS GENERALLY POOR

This shows that, even before developing a disease, smoking has disimproved the quality of life.

WHAT ARE THE MAIN DISEASES ASSOCIATED WITH SMOKING?:

CANCER OF:
- Lung
- Larynx
- Oesophagus(Gullet)
- Stomach
- Bladder
- Lip (Pipe smoking)

Heart Disease
Smokers are twice as likely to die of heart disease as those who don't. Their chances of dying of heart disease are directly associated with the number of cigarettes they smoke.

Stroke
The risk of having a stroke under 55 years of age is increased by 190% by being a smoker. In those over 55 years of age the increase is 80%.

Chronic Bronchitis and Emphysema
These are chronic lung conditions in which there is difficulty in breathing, and recurrent lung infections.

Peptic Ulcer - Duodenal and Stomach Ulcers.
Not alone is smoking associated with an increased incidence of ulcers, but it is also a major factor in preventing them healing, despite modern medication.

Diseases of the Blood Vessels
Smoking is associated with damage to the small blood vessels. This can lead to difficulty in walking due to lack of blood supply to the vessels supplying the calf muscles. If it progresses, it may cause gangrene of the foot, which may require amputation.

Back Pain
Smoking is associated with an increased incidence of back pain. This may be due to increased coughing causing pressure on the back, or smoking interfering with the supply of nutrients (food) to the discs of the back.

A lot of smokers ask, **'Why bother stopping now, I've done all the damage at**

this point'. Stopping at any time produces an improvement in your body.
If you are thirty years' old and give up now, in six months your lungs will be back to a normal appearance and over the years ahead your risk of lung cancer will gradually reduce. At 50 years' of age, your risk will be almost identical to someone who has never smoked. Risk of other diseases shows a similar type of improvement. Those smokers who have suffered a heart attack reduce their chances of another attack by stopping smoking. The reduction in death rate from heart disease in those who give up smoking after a heart attack is remarkable.

HOW DO I STOP?

There are various ways of helping you to stop smoking, but **you must make the decision to stop yourself.** It is not easy and requires considerable effort from you and support from those around you.

IS THERE ANYTHING I SHOULD DO BEFORE STOPPING?

Yes, there are a few tips on the next page which are worth noting. They may help to make kicking the habit a little easier:

1. Get somebody else to give up with you.

2. Learn a relaxation technique - this may help you with those difficult times ahead when you have a craving for a cigarette.

3. The night before you start put away all ash-trays, lighters, matches and cigarettes, of course.

4. Talk with the people you are living with, to enlist their support and help.

5. Decide to give up completely. Cutting down gradually does not work.

ARE THERE ANY AIDS TO HELP ME TO KICK THE HABIT?

NICOTINE CHEWING GUM:

This provides a 'hit' of nicotine when you feel the physical urge for a cigarette.

The **problems** with this method are that :

The chewing gum does not taste very nice;

Most people use it incorrectly. It should be kept in the cheek area without chewing until the urge to smoke is felt. However, a lot of people put the gum in the mouth and keep chewing. This causes an excess of nicotine to be released and you feel quite ill. Effectiveness has not been as good as hoped for.

NICOTINE SKIN PATCHES:

The patch is put on the skin of the thigh or abdomen where it provides a slow release of nicotine into the body. This reduces the physical need for a cigarette. The patch is replaced daily and the best results are achieved if you continue to use them for 12 weeks.

The **problems** with this method are:

Occasional skin rashes;

Expense - to put this in perspective, the daily patch costs the same as 20 cigarettes a day.

The patches are used in conjunction with a booklet and tape which will help with the psychological effects of withdrawal.

HYPNOTHERAPY:

This has been successful for some people, but there are no long term trials of its effectiveness.

ACUPUNCTURE:
>This has been of benefit to some people but again there is no definite proof of its general effectiveness.

NICOTINE NASAL SPRAY:
>This is a new method not yet widely available. Initial results in heavy smokers have been encouraging. The smoker sprays a puff of the liquid up the nose when the urge to smoke comes.

WHILE GIVING UP SMOKING:
>Do not listen to anybody saying "One won't do you any harm.'
>
>If you feel a craving for a cigarette do something. Don't just sit there and think about it.
>
>To help you through these moments use your relaxation technique.

If you still cannot control the craving, think of all the benefits of giving up smoking:

>GENERAL HEALTH
>
>IMPROVED EXERCISE TOLERANCE
>
>IMPROVED BREATH
>
>IMPROVED HEALTH OF THOSE AROUND YOU

Try not to overeat as a substitute for smoking.

>Reduce your coffee/tea intake if you usually smoke with your drink
>
>Eat high fibre foods, so you will feel full and stay away from the table.
>
>Use fruit/vegetables as your substitute, rather than high carbohydrate food.
>
>Eat your normal meals at the usual times and leave the table when finished

DOES PASSIVE SMOKING REALLY AFFECT OTHERS?.

Passive smoking occurs when non-smokers are exposed to smoke through living with a smoker or by inhaling smoke in a social setting. Studies into the effects of passive smoking have shown:

1. AN INCREASE IN RESPIRATORY TRACT INFECTIONS
2. OVER TWICE THE RISK OF LUNG CANCER
3. OVER TWICE THE RISK OF DEATH FROM HEART DISEASE

The more the smoker smokes, the greater the effect on the passive smoker. **Parents should be aware that children who live in a house with a smoker are more likely to:**

1. SUFFER FROM RESPIRATORY TRACT INFECTIONS.
2. SUFFER MORE ASTHMA ATTACKS (IF ASTHMATIC).
3. BECOME SMOKERS THEMSELVES.
4. SUFFER FROM MORE EAR INFECTIONS.

5: ALCOHOL

This is a drug consumed in large quantities throughout the world. Alcohol in moderation is of physical and mental benefit to most people. Recent research shows that a glass of wine a day reduces the risk of heart attacks by 40%. However, consumed to excess, it is responsible for:

1. PHYSICAL DAMAGE TO THE TISSUES OF THE BODY
2. DEPENDENCY - ALCOHOLISM

Alcohol is a depressant. It decreases the speed of reaction to the brain and nervous system by dampening down some of the brain reactions. It produces a nice relaxed feeling. Further alcohol depresses the brain's reactions more, leading to impairment of judgement, coordination and memory.

WHAT PHYSICAL DAMAGE IS CAUSED BY ALCOHOL?

If alcohol's path through the body is followed, it can be seen that taken in excess it can cause damage in most places on its route. Alcohol is taken by mouth, passes through the oesophagus (increased incidence of cancer), into the stomach (increased incidence of gastritis- inflammation of the stomach). It is then carried by the blood vessels through the heart (cardiomyopathy - heart muscle disease), to the brain (intellectual impairment, brain damage) and the other tissues (impotence and many others).

HOW DO I KNOW IF I HAVE AN ALCOHOL ADDICTION?

We all know of people whose lives and families have been ruined by alcohol. The social, financial, and medical effects are catastrophic. A marked feature of alcohol dependency is the inability of the alcoholic to recognise the problem.

DANGER SIGNALS:
DAILY DRINKING;
REGULAR DRINKING TIME, E.G. AFTER WORK;
DRINKING GETTING HEAVIER
ALWAYS BEING THE FIRST PERSON TO FINISH A DRINK;
DRINKING EARLIER IN THE DAY;
DRINKING MORE THAN YOU CAN AFFORD;
DOMESTIC PROBLEMS WITH WIFE OR CHILDREN;
CAR ACCIDENT/LOSS OF DRIVING LICENCE;
MONDAY MORNING ABSENTEEISM;
JOB PROBLEMS/JOB LOSS.

If you feel you have a number of these signals, then at least seek advice from somebody, **excluding your drinking friends**. A real friend, your partner, or your doctor will be able to help. If you are afraid to approach anybody you know, contact your local Alcoholics Anonymous. For those without a dependency problem there are simple guides to sensible drinking. This is a guideline for men as the effects of the same dose of alcohol are worse in women than in men. Regular drinking is more harmful than bout drinking.

WHAT IS MEANT BY SENSIBLE DRINKING?

    1. At least two days a week alcohol-free.

    2. Average consumption should be less than 21 units a week for men.

    1 unit = 1 glass of wine =1/2 pint of beer.

    Do not cheat with the measure

    3. Do not drink during the day.

    4. Do not drink to 'solve your problems'

    5 Do not drink and drive

Chapter 2: STRESS

WHAT IS STRESS?

Stress is any source of pressure that affects the equilibrium or balance of the individual. This pressure can be either physical or mental. The pressure can come from within the person or from a source outside of the person.

IS STRESS HARMFUL?

Stress in itself is not harmful. Everyone needs a level of stress to perform at maximum ability. This level varies from individual to individual. If we look at our friends and relations we find some seem to thrive under extreme pressure while others seem unable to deal with the minor pressures of daily life. Similarly, we have all witnessed sportsmen who 'freeze' on the big occasion and other sportsmen who produce the performance of their lives under maximum pressure. It is therefore our ability to manage, or adapt ourselves to the stress that is important.

WHEN IS STRESS HARMFUL?

Stress is harmful when we lose our ability to respond in a constructive manner to the stress. People who suffer anxiety, or panic attacks as a result of stress, often say "I can't control the attack". It is not that they cannot control the attack, it is that they don't know how.

HOW DO I RECOGNISE THE SIGNS OF STRESS?

The signs of suffering from stress can be divided into two groups.

1. 'obvious' signs.
2. somatising signs

1. 'OBVIOUS' SIGNS

EXCESSIVE TIREDNESS
SLEEP DISTURBANCE
IRRITABILITY
DETERIORATION IN CONCENTRATION
APPETITE DISTURBANCE
LACK OF INTEREST IN SEX
ANXIETY/PANIC ATTACKS

2. SOMATISING SIGNS.

These refer to our ability to transform the mental pressure we are under into physical symptoms. The commoner symptoms are

HEADACHE
NECK/SHOULDER PAIN
MUSCLE PAINS
CHEST PAIN
MOUTH ULCERS
STOMACH UPSET
IRRITABLE BOWEL.SYNDROME
SKIN PROBLEMS

IF YOU FEEL YOU ARE STRESSED WHAT CAN YOU DO ABOUT IT?

The first thing that must be done is to learn how to deal with the stress. This can be achieved through various techniques which help you relax, such as the relaxation techniques described below or Transcendental Meditation. This will help to re-establish your patterns of eating, sleeping and exercising.

Following the re-establishment of normal patterns in your life it is then time to sit back and examine how you became so stressed. It may be that you have simply taken on too much or that your way of life needs to be altered to deal with the stress. Sometimes your inability to cope may point to a deeper disturbance in yourself. You may be unaware of the problem causing this disturbance, as you may have 'blocked out' the problem, particularly if it was a traumatic experience in your childhood.

Relaxation techniques.

Relaxation techniques are easy to learn.
The first thing is to find a place where you are comfortable and unlikely to be disturbed. Loosen any tight clothing.
To relax, you need to be aware of what you are trying to do without striving to make it happen. Try the breathing exercises below to see if you are going about it the right way:

BREATHING

Breathing correctly is critical for correct relaxation. To see if you are breathing correctly, put your right hand over your chest and your left hand over your abdomen [tummy]. Take a deep breath in slowly. If the right hand on the chest, is moving first, you are breathing incorrectly. Try again and focus on the abdomen moving first.
Once you have achieved this, gradually slow down your breathing rate, without pausing between breathing in and breathing out. You may find it helpful to think of the word 'calm' while breathing out.

MUSCLE RELAXATION.

This involves focusing on a muscle group, eg the muscles of the hands, tensing the muscle group and then relaxing those muscles. By relaxing in this way we become aware of the feeling of tension in the muscles, and by being aware, are able to relax the tense muscles.

SHOULDERS AND NECK.

Lying down on your back, lift your head off the ground. Hold for five seconds. Now relax, slowly lowering your head back onto the ground. Now press your shoulders down into the floor. Count to five and relax.

If sitting, shrug your shoulders as hard as you can. Count to five and then drop your shoulders and relax.

FACE

Tighten the muscles of your face, as if frowning, and close your eyes as tightly as you can. Again hold for a count of five and relax. Keep your eyelids resting gently against each other.

MOUTH

Clench your jaw tightly, count to five and relax.

BODY

Relax your body, firstly by inhaling deeply and holding your breath. Tighten your abdominal muscles. Hold for a count of five and exhale suddenly. Feel yourself relaxing.

PELVIS AND LEGS

While lying down squeeze your buttocks together. Now lift your buttocks off the ground, hold for five and relax. Keep your two legs together and stretch them out. Keep your toes pointed. Hold for five and relax.

Do the exercises and then repeat them. Continue for about ten minutes. If, after this time, you still feel a muscle group is tense, tense them fully and then relax. Stay lying down and enjoy the feeling.

If you find your mind is still agitated, let yourself create a soothing image, such as lying on a beach with the sun beating down. Once you have the image in your mind, focus on feeling the pleasurable sensations associated with the image. Feel the warmth of the sun on your body and the warm sand under you. Smell the sea air and listen to the waves gently breaking on the shore. This will allow your mind to relax.

If you find unwanted thoughts entering your mind, don't get excited. Just be aware of their presence and let your mind return to the pleasurable image you have created. Try to relax like this for a few minutes.

Once you have learned these techniques, can use them regularly to reduce your tension. In addition, if you find yourself feeling stressed, you can do a quick relaxation by tensing all the muscles of the body, counting to five and then relaxing the whole body.

You can also prepare yourself for stressful situations by allowing yourself to think of the situation while thinking of your pleasurable image after relaxing. The difficult situation can thereby become associated with this image. This often decreases the stress when the situation arises.
Using these will allow you to re-establish your normal patterns of sleeping, eating, exercise etc.

Work-related stress.

Most men experience stress associated with work. Often this is helpful in getting work finished, for instance for a deadline. However, a lot of men experience excessive stress at work because of **poor time management.** They often feel they have too much to do and not enough time to do it in. To assess how you are using time, firstly **itemise in order of priority** the jobs you have in hand. Secondly, **arrange to keep a time-log**. This is a record of what you are actually doing every half hour. Analysis of the time-log in combination with the priority listing will allow you to see not alone where you are spending your time but whether you are using your actual working time on the right items of work. You will also **know how long a given task takes**, and be able to **organise accordingly.**

Having studied this you can then arrange your work so that high priority items receive an appropriate amount of time. You can also assess what **tasks can be delegated.** Instead of feeling that "if you want something done properly then you have to do it yourself", find the best person available to do the job. It is important to tell them exactly what you want done. Now **leave him alone and let him/her do the job**. Don't forget to thank him/her when the job is finished. This improves working relationships, which will help to reduce stress.

Arrange to **take short breaks** during the working day. A break of ten minutes in the morning and ten minutes in the afternoon is sufficient. Try to relax or even snooze during the break. You will return to work refreshed and will work more efficiently as a result.

You must also **develop the ability to say no**. If you haven't the time for a particular job, then there is no advantage to anyone in your taking it on in the first place.

Make proper time for leisure. Leisure is not just something to be added on to your day. Plan the time you need for leisure and use it properly. Don't just let the time pass by.

Chapter 3: Heart Disease.

Heart attacks are the single most common cause of death in the western world. Ischaemic heart disease is the most common cause of this.

The heart is the body's pump. It pumps around the blood which carries fuel to the body's tissues.

Ischaemic means lack of sufficient blood supply, causing reduction in the supply of oxygen and other essential 'fuels' to the tissues. When this lack of oxygen affects the heart it causes damage to the heart muscle. Tight chest pain [Angina] can be a warning that the muscle is being damaged. When the person stops exerting himself this pain will usually settle. If there is no warning or the person doesn't heed the warning, or if the pain persists despite rest, part of the heart muscle may die.resulting in a heart attack or myocardial infarction. The consequences of the death of heart muscle depends upon :

    a) How much heart muscle dies
    b) Which part of the muscle dies.

The heart has an 'electrical' system and if a 'Main Junction" in this system dies, the heart may stop beating.

WHAT CAUSES ISCHAEMIC HEART DISEASE?

Ischaemic heart disease is usually caused by blockage of the arteries which supply blood to the heart's muscles. This happens because of damage to the blood vessel wall. The body tries to fix this damaged wall but its patching-up gradually blocks up the artery with a porridge-like sludge called atheroma. This can block-off the artery at that point. Alternatively, a small piece of the sludge can break off and this small clot then swims off and, as the artery gets smaller, it gets stuck. This blocks the

artery and therefore blood-flow past that point.
The ideal form of treatment should therefore be to prevent damage to the blood vessels.

WHAT ARE THE RISK FACTORS FOR HEART DISEASE?

1. Gender

    Being male increases your chances of heart disease and the outcome for a man with heart disease is worse than that for a woman with heart disease.

2. Age

    The incidence of heart disease increases with age and the outlook is worse in the elderly.

3. Family history of sudden deaths or heart disease.

The main feature of these three major risk factors is the we can do nothing about them, i.e. they cannot be altered. However, the factors below can be altered with lifestyle and/or treatment.

4. High blood cholesterol.
5. High blood-pressure..
6. Smoking.
7. Diabetes.

All of these show a strong association with heart disease. They are all capable of damaging the blood vessel wall.
The factors listed below have a weak association with heart disease.

8. Overweight.
9. Lack of exercise.
10. Stress.

11. Gout.
12. Alcohol excess.

As can be seen from this list, it is clear that in most cases of heart disease there are a number of factors at work in producing the disease. It is also true that we don't know all the risk factors as of yet.

Cholesterol

The single most important adjustable factor in the prevention of heart disease. There is no country in the world with a high incidence of heart disease where the average cholesterol of the population is low.

WHAT IS CHOLESTEROL?

Cholesterol is one of the fats of the body. We all have a certain level of cholesterol in our body. Certain families have a naturally high cholesterol. Most of these families have a higher incidence of heart disease

In addition to our natural level of cholesterol, we eat cholesterol in our diet. Particular foods have a high cholesterol, such as dairy produce and eggs.

HOW DOES CHOLESTEROL CAUSE HEART DISEASE?

Cholesterol is thought to cause heart disease by damaging the blood vessel wall. This appears to happen because the cholesterol causes the formation of a hyperactive particle called a free radical which is capable of damaging the cells lining the blood vessel. Once these cells are damaged, it sets in train the body's repair system, but unfortunately this causes a patch to form on the damage. This patch then causes flow problems in the blood stream, similar to a stone in a stream. Unfortunately this flow problem leads to the patch getting bigger as bits get stuck onto it. It gradually causes the blood vessel to get blocked-off.

Different countries have differing average cholesterol levels in their populations. When the hugely varying death-rate from heart disease in various countries is compared with the average cholesterol from the same countries, a close symmetry is found. In countries where there has been a reduction in the average cholesterol level, there has been a corresponding fall in deaths from heart-disease.

It is estimated that a 1% fall in blood cholesterol produces a 2% fall in deaths from heart disease.

It is interesting to note that certain vitamins reduce the concentration of the hyperactive free radicals that cause the damage to the heart's blood vessels. These vitamins, in particular Vitamin C, Vitamin E and Beta-carotene, have been shown to have a protective effect on the heart. Vitamin C is found in most fresh fruit and vegetables, in particular citrus fruits. Beta carotene is found in carrots and other fresh vegetables. Vitamin E is an oil soluble vitamin, found in high concentration in olive oil. This protective effect may explain the low incidence of heart-disease in those countries with a 'Mediterranean diet'.

WHO SHOULD HAVE THEIR BLOOD CHOLESTEROL CHECKED?

1. Family History

People with a strong history in their families of heart disease or sudden premature death should definitely have their cholesterol checked by their General Practitioner or at a recognised clinic. Also those with a family history of high blood fats.

2. Those under drug treatment for high blood-pressure.
3. Everyone with diabetes.
4. With known heart disease - even those who have had a heart attack or a by-pass.
5. Those with signs on examination by their doctor of possible high blood fats.

The checking of blood cholesterol on the High Street is not of any benefit as :
1. A lot of the instruments are inaccurate - your doctor will have to check it again.
2. There is no follow-up - for all these risk factors, change in lifestyle must be long-term. Being handed a diet sheet without discussion of the individual's own diet seems to be of little use and unlikely to be successful.

For most of us, simple alteration in our diet can produce huge improvements in our cholesterol.

1. Reduce butter, cream and cheese - stopping them altogether causes a 10% reduction in cholesterol.
2. Change to low-fat produce - milk/yoghurt
3. Cut fat off meat.
4. Eat more fish.
5. Do not fry food
6. Stop eating biscuits, cakes, ice-cream, chocolate and pastries
7. Eat more fresh fruit and fresh vegetables - not alone do they reduce your appetite for other foods, but they also have a protective effect from the adverse effects of cholesterol.

There is really no point in getting your cholesterol checked if these alterations are beyond you.

WHAT TREATMENT WILL I GET IF MY CHOLESTEROL IS HIGH?

Firstly your doctor will probably repeat the test. If the result is very high he may take the sample after you have been fasting for 14 hours. This will allow him to get a break-down of your cholesterol into three different types. The ratio between two of these types is important in assessing whether you need treatment at all, and if you do - what treatment should be started.

For most people treatment with a cholesterol lowering diet will be sufficient. This will be discussed with you by your doctor or dietician. They will suggest starting the diet and will arrange to check the cholesterol level after three months. There is not much point in checking the blood cholesterol before then, as it takes that long for the diet to be effective.

If you have a cholesterol in a higher range, or if your cholesterol has failed to improve, your doctor may introduce medication in addition to your diet.

High Blood-pressure.

High blood-pressure has been known to have an association with heart-disease for a long time. Unfortunately, while medical treatment of high blood-pressure has been successful at preventing strokes, there has not been a similar improvement in prevention of heart-disease. This is possibly because the older families of drugs we have been using had an adverse effect on the blood fats. Hopefully, the newer families of anti-blood pressure tablets will show a reduction in heart disease.

HOW DO I PREVENT HIGH BLOOD-PRESSURE?
1. No salt added to cooking or food.
2. Weight reduction - if overweight. [See chart Page ...]
3. Increased exercise.
4. Moderate alcohol consumption.

Smoking.

Smoking in males shows a direct relationship between the number of cigarettes smoked and the risk of developing ischaemic heart disease. On average, smokers are more than twice as likely to die of heart-disease. [See smoking chapter].

Exercise.

Exercise is beneficial to the heart. Even people already suffering from heart-disease or recovering from a heart-attack or a by-pass benefit from exercise. Exercise both benefits the heart by its general effects of burning up excess calories and also has a direct beneficial effect on the heart's muscles. It increases the efficiency of the heart's muscle, so that it requires less oxygen to do a specific task. This means that even in the presence of heart disease, the muscle can do more without being damaged.

SHOULD I CONSULT MY DOCTOR ABOUT EXERCISING?
If you have a history of heart-disease your doctor should be consulted before starting an exercise

programme. If you have had a heart-attack or by-pass, an exercise-tolerance test is necessary before starting. If you get chest pain while exercising, you should stop and see your doctor as soon as possible.

HOW MUCH EXERCISE DO I NEED TO DO FOR IT TO BE OF BENEFIT?

To be beneficial, exercise must be regular, last for at least twenty minutes, and be sufficiently strenuous to increase your pulse rate.

4: Cancer.

WHAT IS CANCER?

Cancer is an overgrowth of the body's tissues, which usually starts with one abnormal cell, which then replicates and forms the cancer.

The cancer is benign if the growth does not invade other tissues.

Cancers are usually slow-growing and only cause problems if :
1. They press on important structures, i.e. brain.
2. They produce hormones, i.e. thyroid adenoma

A malignant cancer is usually rapidly growing and is invasive of other tissues.

Some cancers can be prevented by alteration in lifestyle :
1. STOP SMOKING [SEE CHAPTER 1]
2. REDUCE ALCOHOL [SEE CHAPTER 1]
3. INCREASE FIBRE IN DIET [SEE CHAPTER 1]
4. REDUCE EXPOSURE TO SUN.

4. Reduce exposure to sun.

This has always been advisable, but recent changes in our environment have made it mandatory. The reduction in the ozone layer is allowing increasing amounts of radiation to filter through from the sun. This increases the incidence of skin cancer.

The increase in the incidence of skin cancer is 2-3%.for every 1% reduction in the ozone layer. In particular there has been a major increase in the incidence of malignant melanoma, the most potentially lethal of the three common forms of skin cancer. A recent survey in Dublin showed a doubling of the incidence of malignant melanomas over the last five years. The incidence was found to be particularly high in those who work indoors and then have intensive sun holidays.

HOW MUCH SUN CAN I TAKE?

If your skin is red at the end of a day in the sun then you have been over-exposed.

The amount of sun necessary to cause redness varies according to
- skin type.
- exposure during 'peak' hours [11a.m-3p.m]
- the length of time exposed to the sun
- the use of sun protection factors

SKIN TYPE

There is a marked increase in the incidence of skin cancer in those with so-called celtic skin.in particular when they emigrate to warmer climates. Ireland for instance has the highest incidence of malignant melanoma for its latitude. They are usually fair or red haired. Having blue eyes is also associated with increased burning. The incidence in black people is much lower. Skin types are therefore divided into six groups between these two extremes.

SKIN TYPES

1. Fair white skin which burns very easily and never tans
2. Fair white skin which burns at first but eventually develops a tan
3. White skin that tans.easily and rarely burns
4. Mediterranean skin that tans very easily and never burns
5. Brown skin
6. Black afro-caribbean skin.

SUNBLOCKS IN STRONG SUNLIGHT.

Type 1	Use full sun block [factor 25] on initial exposure .you can gradually reduce to factor 12
Type 2-4	Start with factor 15 and gradually reduce to factor 6-8.
Type 5-6	Don't need sunscreen may need moisturiser to prevent skin drying out.

WHAT ARE THE RULES FOR AVOIDING SUNBURN?

1. Wear a T-shirt and hat. They are effective sunblocks.

2. Use sunblock creams

3. Be very careful at the start of your holiday. Ration your exposure to the sun at this stage of your holiday.

4. Do not sunbathe during the peak hours of sunlight [11a.m-3p.m.]

5. Protect children's skin. sunburn in childhood is associated with increased incidence of skin cancer in adulthood

Go to your doctor if you notice any of these changes in your skin:

A) CHANGE IN THE SIZE OF A MOLE, FRECKLE OR SKIN LUMP

B) CHANGE IN THE COLOUR OF A MOLE, FRECKLE OR SKIN LUMP

c) CHANGE IN THE SHAPE OF THE ABOVE, IN PARTICULAR IF THE EDGE HAS BECOME IRREGULAR
d) ITCHINESS OF A MOLE, FRECKLE OR SKIN LUMP
e) A BREAK IN THE SURFACE OF THE SKIN.
f) BLEEDING FROM A SKIN MOLE, FRECKLE OR LUMP

With any form of skin cancer the outlook is excellent with early detection and treatment. Late presentation with a change on your skin can be fatal, if it turns out you have a malignant melanoma.

The statement regarding early presentation, diagnosis and treatment of skin cancers also applies to other cancers. Symptoms that you should get early medical advice for include:

1. UNPLANNED WEIGHT LOSS.
2. UNEXPLAINED BLEEDING - BLOOD IN YOUR BOWEL MOTION, BLOOD IN THE URINE, COUGHING UP BLOOD.
3. PERSISTENCE OF ANY UNUSUAL SYMPTOM, E.G. COUGH, HOARSENESS, DIARRHOEA.

Chapter 5: WELL MAN ADVICE

Men are lucky. They do not have a monthly cycle whereby they have to suffer physical and mental changes associated with changing hormone levels. Fortunately, the male hormone levels remain reasonably stable.after puberty. Men are also lucky in that they don't get a sudden fall off in hormones, as women do with the menopause.

In addition, men also have the advantage that the male sex organs are not hidden away. Most of us can see and feel our testes [testicles] and penis. This makes it easier for us to discover if there is something wrong with either.

WHAT SHOULD WE BE CONCERNED ABOUT AS MEN?
1. TESTES [TESTICLES] PROBLEMS
2. PENIS PROBLEMS
3. PROSTATE PROBLEMS
4. SEXUALLY-TRANSMITTED DISEASE [SEE CHAPTER 9]

HOW DOES THE SYSTEM WORK?

Basically sperm is produced in the testes, matures in the epididymis and is then pumped up in the vas deferens to the prostate gland. There the sperm is mixed with additional fluid [which is needed to help the sperm get to the female egg]. When the male reaches a climax this is then pumped out through the erect penis.

WHY ARE THE TESTES HANGING DOWN IN A SACK?

The testes hang down in a sack because sperm can only be produced when the temperature is lower than the normal body temperature.

To get a clear understanding of these problems, it's a good idea to have a guide to the local geography. Please see map below.

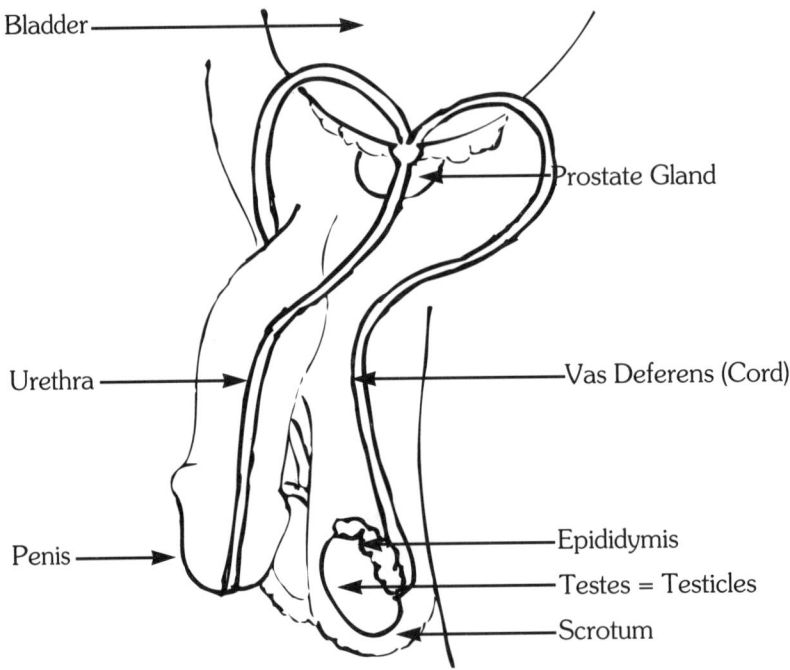

1. Testes problems.

Women are told to examine their breasts, so why aren't men told to examine their testes?

SELF-EXAMINATION OF YOUR TESTES:

Examining your testes is a relatively easy thing to do. Firstly, because they are hanging down in a sack and secondly, because there is only skin between your fingers and the testes. If you get used to the way your testes normally feel, you will then notice any change quickly.

WHY BOTHER EXAMINING THEM?

Cancer of the testes is the most common cancer in men between the age of 29 and 34. Fortunately, it is still an uncommon cancer, but early detection leads to virtually a one hundred per cent cure rate.

HOW DO I EXAMINE THEM?

The best time to examine the testes is after a bath or a shower, as the skin of the scrotum is softer at that time.

Place your thumb at the top of the testes. Now place your index and middle fingers at the bottom of the testes. Roll the testes backwards and forwards, then roll it sideways. Repeat the examination on the other testes.

At the top of the testes you will feel a knobbly bit where the cord meets the testes. This is called the epididymis. The testes itself is usually egg-shaped. It is generally firm with a smooth surface.

WHAT DO I DO IF I FIND A SWELLING?

The general advice would be to see your doctor. The first thing to know is that most lumps in the scrotum [sac] are not cancerous.

When examining the testes, if you find there is a swelling above your thumb, in other words above your testes, it could be a swelling of:
The cord
The epididymis

Tackling Men's Health

The veins of the scrotum
A hernia coming down from the groin
These are discussed below.

PAINFUL TESTES : ACUTE [SUDDEN] ONSET OF PAIN.

Questions :
Did you receive any **injury** to your testes in the last 2 days?

Did you have **mumps** recently?

If the answer to both questions is no, contact your doctor immediately. **You may have a twisted testes [torsion of testes].**
This is an emergency, because, unless dealt with urgently, the blood supply to testes is cut off and the testes will die.

INJURY:

If your testes have become swollen or tender after an injury [kick during sport], contact your doctor immediately. Usually bed rest and pain relief is sufficient, but occasionally an operation is necessary.

MUMPS:

Mumps can cause swelling of one or both of your testes. This is usually painful. The treatment is rest and pain relief. Unfortunately, if mumps develops after puberty, it may lead to infertility. This is one of the reasons why all children are offered vaccination against mumps at 15 months [MMR].
Contact your doctor if you have mumps.

OTHER CAUSES OF PAINFUL TESTES:
Epididymo-orchitis.
This is infection of the epididymis - the knobbly bit at the top of the testes. It is usually treated with rest and antibiotics. Occasionally this may be due to T.B..

PAINLESS LUMPS ABOVE THE TESTES:
Hernia
Cyst of cord
Varicocele
Cyst of Epididymis/Spermatocele

HERNIA

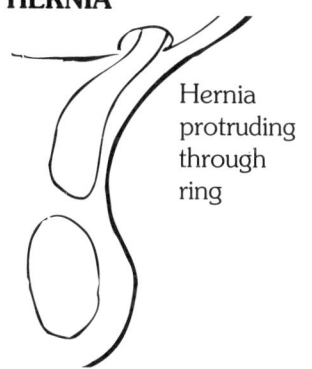

Hernia protruding through ring

A hernia is a pouch containing intestine or other contents of the abdomen which has pushed out through a defect in the wall of the abdomen.

This may track down into the scrotum, alongside the vas deferens [spermatic cord]. Most hernias will go back into the abdomen on lying down. Some need a little push to do so. If, however, the hernia does not go back on lying down, or with an upward push on lying down, or if the hernia becomes painful, consult your doctor as soon as possible.

WHAT IS THE TREATMENT?

Surgery is the only definitive treatment. Almost all hernias in the groin can be operated on, even if the man is unfit for a full anaesthetic.

WHAT HAPPENS IF I JUST LEAVE IT THERE?

The danger is that the neck of the hernia pouch can get too tight. If this happens the blood supply to the pouch and its contents is cut off. The contents of the sac then die with ensuing gangrene of the intestine within the sac. This is called a strangulated hernia and 10 - 15% of people with strangulated hernias die.

CYST OF THE CORD

A cyst of the cord (vas deferens) is a small fluid-filled sac. This can be confirmed by an ultrasound scan or by taking fluid from the cyst.
It does not require treatment unless it enlarges and becomes uncomfortable.

VARICOCELE

If there is a swelling which looks and feels like a bag of worms, this is a varicocele. A varicocele is varicose veins of the veins to the testes.
To confirm that your swelling is a varicocele, lie down and lift your scrotum up. The swelling should almost disappear, as the veins have drained. A varicocele is usually on the left side.

IF YOU HAVE A VARICOCELE, IS IT IMPORTANT??

Yes, is the short answer. As noted above, the reason the testes are hanging down in a sac is to keep them cool. If you have a varicocele, the extra blood that is pooled in the scrotum increases the temperature around the testes. Sperm production is therefore decreased or stopped altogether.

WHAT IS THE TREATMENT?

Surgery is the only treatment.

CYST OF THE EPIDIDYMIS.

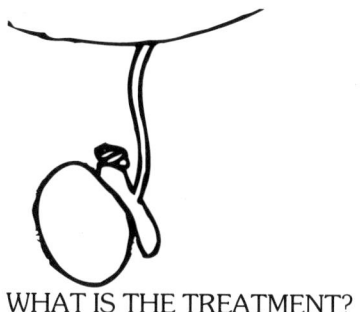

The knobbly bit at the top of the testes is called the epididymis. A non tender swelling here is usually a cyst. This can be confirmed by ultrasound scan or by a doctor taking fluid from the cyst. Sometimes the fluid from the cyst is white like barley water. The fluid contains sperm and the cyst is therefore called a spermatocele.

WHAT IS THE TREATMENT?

The fluid can be taken from the cyst, but the cyst may reform. Minor surgery may be necessary if there is frequent recurrence, or if the cyst becomes uncomfortable.

IF THERE IS GENERALISED, PAINLESS SWELLING OF THE SCROTUM, WHAT IS THE LIKELY CAUSE?

A hydrocele.

WHAT IS **A HYDROCELE**?

A hydrocele is a collection of fluid between the layers that cover the testes. An easy way to confirm this is by applying a pocket torch to the skin behind the testes. If the swelling is a hydrocele, the light will shine through this fluid-filled sac [transillumination].

WHAT IS THE TREATMENT?

The hydrocele can be drained under local anaesthetic. With frequent recurrence surgical treatment may be necessary. If you have recently developed a hydrocele it is advisable to have it checked by your doctor, as on occasion, it may be hiding something more sinister.

Swellings of the testes itself should be seen by your doctor as soon as possible. Cancer of the testes is virtually 100% curable with early detection. Therefore, get into the habit of examining your testes after a bath or a shower. If you feel something abnormal get it seen to.

NO TESTES:

If there is no testes on one side of the scrotum, then it is necessary to ask two questions :

1. Is there a testes?
2. If there is a testes, where is it?

Occasionally there may be no testes. More commonly the testes may have got stuck during its descent from the abdomen [tummy] to the scrotum. [This descent happens during development in the womb]. This is called an undescended testes.

WHY BOTHER FINDING AN UNDESCENDED TESTES?

1. If found in the groin during childhood, the undescended testes can, as a rule, be brought down into the scrotum [sack]. The best time for this operation to be performed is around five years of age.

2. If the testes is not found or if it is not brought down into the scrotum, then testes development is abnormal. This may lead to:

   a) Infertility - As the temperature is higher out of the scrotum, the testes does not produce sperm. Unfortunately, not alone does the undescended testes fail to produce sperm but it also causes a reaction in the body which interferes with the sperm producing cells of the normal testes. This may lead to problems with fertility.

b) Cancer - There is an increased incidence of cancer of the testes in untreated undescended testes. This again is felt to be due to the unusual environment the testes is in, although on occasion the testes has failed to descend because it was abnormal to start with.

If the testes is discovered to be undescended after childhood, surgical removal is recommended as:

The testes will not produce sperm at this stage.

It may be interfering with sperm production in the other normal testes
It may become cancerous.

2: Penis problems

The penis is involved in both excretion of urine and sexual functions. Therefore problems with the penis, such as pain, arise from the urinary tract or may be local to the penis. The local problems will be dealt with in this section.

1. FORESKIN PROBLEMS
2. GLANS PROBLEMS
3. ERECTION PROBLEMS
4. LUMPS, SORES, BLISTERS, ULCERS (SEE SECTION ON SEXUALLY TRANSMITTED DISEASES)

1. FORESKIN PROBLEMS

The foreskin is the fold of skin covering the tip of the penis. It should be easy to roll back to expose the top of the penis, known as the Glans. If this can be done, you should maintain the hygiene of the area by drawing back the skin and cleaning under the foreskin with mild soap and water while in the bath or shower. Not doing this may lead to

Infection
Cancer of the penis

If the skin cannot be drawn back easily then circumcision should be considered. This should be done for two reasons

To facilitate cleaning
To prevent problems with erection

WHAT IS CIRCUMCISION?

An operation in which the foreskin is removed by cutting it away at the bottom of the glans. This is done under a general (full) anaesthetic.

WILL THIS AFFECT MY SEX LIFE?

No, once fully healed after the operation, it does not appear to affect the sensitivity of the glans or affect orgasm in any way.

2. GLANS PROBLEMS
PAINFUL GLANS

Is it red or swollen?
Does the pain happen during intercourse only?
Does the pain occur after intercourse only?

RED OR SWOLLEN GLANS:

Infection is the usual cause. It is called balanitis and can be treated with local or oral antibiotics. See your doctor for treatment and assessment of whether any further intervention is necessary.

PENIS PAIN DURING INTERCOURSE.

This may be a problem with lubrication. Ask your partner about similar discomfort. This may be the result of inadequate foreplay leading to penetration of vagina before it is adequately lubricated. (Foreplay is the sensual arousal of each other's bodies before penetrative sex). The lack of lubrication causes friction with intercourse, leading to pain. Sometimes it is necessary to use a lubricant jelly. These can be bought over the counter in a pharmacy.

PENIS PAIN AFTER INTERCOURSE.

The possibilities here are an allergic reaction or, less commonly, an infection. The reaction may be due to the method of contraception. Examples of this are allergy to the rubber in condoms, allergy to the spermicidal creams, or allergy to the solution in which a diaphragm is cleaned.

Trying an alternative method of contraception may be worthwhile. If this fails, and you cannot find another cause, consult your doctor.

ERECTION PROBLEMS.

Some men experience pain with an erection. Painful erection can be divided into two groupings:

PAINFUL ERECTION IN WHICH THE PENIS REMAINS ERECT WITHOUT SEXUAL STIMULUS:

Contact your doctor immediately. The veins of the penis cannot drain. This needs to be seen immediately or permanent problems may develop. The condition is called priapism.

PAINFUL ERECTION WHERE THE ERECTION GOES AWAY ON REMOVAL OF THE SEXUAL STIMULUS.

The foreskin being too tight is usually the problem. Circumcision may be necessary.

If, during sexual activity, the foreskin has been pulled back, and afterwards it is not possible to draw it back over the glans (top) of the penis, you should see a doctor. If it does not come back easily, continuing to try to bring it back will cause swelling. This makes the problem worse and creates a tight band at the bottom of the glans. Your doctor may be able to get the foreskin back in place. Where this cannot be done, it may be necessary to release the tight band by operation. This usually occurs in the sexually inexperienced where the man fails to bring his foreskin back after sexual activity.

3: Prostate Problems.

The prostate is a chestnut-shaped gland situated at the base of the bladder. It encircles the urethra (the outflow pipe from the bladder). This is important to the understanding of the symptoms it produces. Its function is to produce fluid which mixes with sperm coming up in the vas to become semen - the fluid a man releases at orgasm.

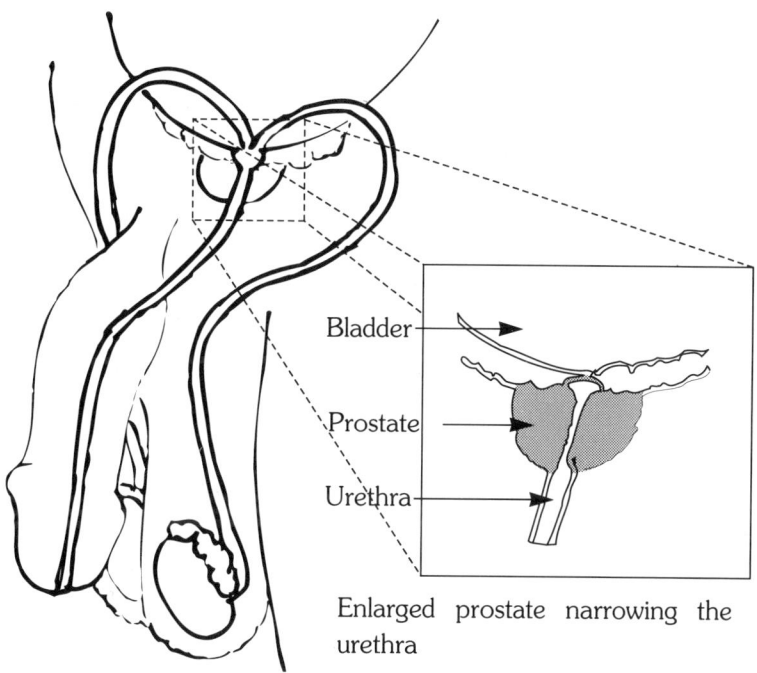

Enlarged prostate narrowing the urethra

1. PROSTATITIS

This is infection of the prostate gland. The usual complaint with this is pain on passing urine. You may also complain of pain between the legs on passing urine. Fever is usually a symptom.

WHAT IS THE TREATMENT?

Go to your doctor with a fresh urine sample. Following examination of you and your urine he will advise treatment, usually rest and antibiotics.

2. PROSTATE ENLARGEMENT

a) Benign prostatic hypertrophy
b) Prostatic cancer

As discussed above the prostate encircles the outflow tube from the bladder. Therefore if the prostate gets bigger, it blocks the outflow of urine from the bladder. This produces symptoms which can be divided into two groups:

1. OBSTRUCTION SYMPTOMS:
   a) Difficulty starting to urinate – extra pressure needed
   b) Poor stream of urine - difficulty urinating against a wall
   c) Feeling that the bladder is not empty when finished urinating
   d) Dribbling at the end of urinating
   e) Complete obstruction of outflow - known as Acute Retention - this produces severe lower abdominal pain

2. IRRITATIVE SYMPTOMS -
   The bladder muscle becomes irritated at not being able to empty and becomes over-active resulting in:

   a) Frequent urination at night time disturbing sleep

b) Frequent urination day-time

c) Urgent desire to pass urine, but little or no urine passed.

d) Urgent desire to pass urine and unable to get to the toilet in time resulting in bedwetting (incontinence).

WHAT WILL MY GP DO WHEN I TELL HIM MY SYMPTOMS?

1. Examination including back passage finger exam. The prostate can be felt through the back passage and your doctor will get a good idea of its size. It will also help him assess whether the enlargement is more likely to be benign or prostatic cancer

2. Urine test to check for infection, which may occur due to the stagnation of urine in the bladder

3. Blood tests

a) to assess whether there has been any damage to the kidney

b) to assess whether the enlargement is more likely to be cancer of the prostate or otherwise.

WHAT WILL HAPPEN AFTER THIS?

He will probably refer you to a specialist who will further assess the situation. He will take x-rays/scans, do a urine flow assessment and possibly an examination under anaesthetic.

WHO GETS BENIGN PROSTATIC HYPERTROPHY?

Nearly every man over the age of 55 will have some degree of enlargement of the prostate. This enlargement may not cause any symptoms, as it is not interfering with outflow. Most men, however, will have mild symptoms, such as needing extra pressure to start urinating or having to get up once at night. If symptoms are worse and the bladder is not emptying there will be back pressure on the kidneys. This can lead to serious problems.

WHAT TREATMENT IS AVAILABLE?

1. Medication. Tablets are useful in a small percentage of people. These are men who are unfit for surgery, or where surgery has been deferred, or men.who are awaiting surgery.

2. Surgery.

There are two types of surgery.in common use at present:

a Transurethral resection. This is done through a type of telescope inserted through the penis under a full anaesthetic. Almost all benign prostates are removed using this procedure.

b. Through the abdomen. This involves a skin wound in the stomach wall.

ARE THERE ANY COMPLICATIONS AFTER PROSTATE SURGERY?

Retrograde ejaculation.

Some men complain that their semen ejaculation does not occur after the operation. They are ejaculating, but unfortunately their ejaculation goes back into the bladder. This semen is then passed when they next urinate.

Impotence.

This is becoming less common with improved operative techniques.

Incontinence.

This is an infrequent complication. It occurs in less than 2%.of men after transurethral removal of the prostate.

A.new technique has become available recently. This involves a special catheter or tube being guided to the prostate, through the penis. Microwave waves are then emitted from the tip of this catheter. The heat from these waves shrinks the prostate causing an improvement in flow.

The **advantages** of this technique are

1. It can be performed as a day patient in hospital and there is a possible reduced incidence of complications associated with the other surgical procedures
2. This technique is called Transurethral Microwave Thermotherapy, and is still being fully assessed.

PROSTATIC CANCER

WHO GETS CANCER OF THE PROSTATE?

Prostate cancer is rare under the age of sixty. However, in men over sixty, it is now the commonest form of cancer. A man has a one in ten chance of developing prostate cancer. A third of those will die as a result of it.

IS IT TREATABLE?

Yes. Treatment may involve surgical removal of the prostate and/or hormone therapy. The earlier it is picked up the better. If noticed early, before it has spread to other areas of the body i.e. bone secondaries, the prostate is removed. If, however, there has been a spread there is treatment which blocks the production of male sex hormones.

Prostate cancer is stimulated by the production of male sex hormones, so by decreasing the male sex hormone you decrease the stimulation of the prostate cancer. Occasionally, where hormone treatment is unsuccessful, both testes are removed by a surgeon to stop male hormone production.

HOW CAN IT BE DETECTED EARLY?

If you present with symptoms of prostate trouble there is a blood test your doctor can do which will tell if there is a likelihood of prostatic cancer

CAN YOU PREVENT IT HAPPENING?

At present, no. There has been a large increase of prostate cancer over the last twenty years but nobody has found a definite reason for that increase.

IF PROSTATE CANCER IS SO COMMON THEN WHY ISN'T THERE SCREENING FOR IT?

This is a major item for discussion at present. Research into prostatic cancer is poorly funded in comparison with more high profile cancers such as breast cancer, possibly as a result of it arising in a more elderly population. The other reason is that the blood test that is currently available, the prostatic specific antigen (PSA) is a reasonably new test that detects prostate cancer earlier and more specifically than the blood test previously used. There are specialists suggesting that all men over 50 years of age have yearly:

1. RECTAL EXAMINATION

    A finger examination of the back passage. The doctor can feel the prostate reasonably easily this way. The enlargement of the prostate in benign prostate enlargement occurs usually in a different part of the prostate gland than prostate cancer.

2. BLOOD TEST.

Prostate Specific Antigen is an excellent test which may detect prostatic cancer early. Some specialists have recommended its use in screening for prostate cancer.

Chapter 6: Male infertility

This affects over 10% of couples. The incidence seems to be rising, probably as a result of later marriages or because many couples choose to delay starting a family. Another factor is the increased sexual activity before marriage. More sexual partners leads to increased sexually-transmitted disease which may affect male or female fertility.

30% of cases of infertility are due to problems with the male alone, 30% of cases.are due to problems with the female alone, and the remaining 40% are due to problems with both the male and the female

Normal reproduction in men.

Sperm are produced in the testes (testicles). Two hormones are necessary for this. Testosterone and FSH. The.sperm mature in the epididymis. They are then pumped up the Vas Deferens to the Prostate where additional fluid is added to help the sperm reach the female's egg. The sperm is then pumped out through the urethra. There is usually more than 100 million sperm released into the vagina in the ejaculation. Only one sperm, however, joins with the egg.

WHAT INCREASES THE SPERM COUNT?
1. Good general health
2. Good diet with plenty of fresh fruit and vegetables, Vitamin C, Vitamin B12
3. Wearing loose non-nylon underwear (cotton is best). This keeps the testicles.cooler than the body temperature. Production is better at lower temperatures.
4. Avoid hot baths, saunas, steam rooms, particularly prior to intercourse.

WHAT DECREASES THE SPERM COUNT?
1. Smoking
2. Alcohol -more than 3 pints or equivalent a day

Tackling Men's Health

3. Medication, e.g.:
   a) Cimetidine (Tagamet)
   b) Some anti-depressants
   c) Nitrofurantoin (Furadantin)
   d) Salazopyrin (Colitis treatment)

Consult your GP if on any medication

4. Illness
5. Drugs - Marijuana, Heroin/Morphine
6. Occupation - for example welders working at 1.5 degrees above body temperature have been shown to have a lower sperm count.

DOES ABSTINENCE IMPROVE SPERM COUNT?
No

DOES MASTURBATION ADVERSELY AFFECT SPERM COUNT?
No

DOES 'EXCESSIVE' INTERCOURSE CAUSE INFERTILITY?
No

The causes of male infertility can be divided into groups. These groups are logical, if we understand the normal reproduction in a man.

1. Problems with production of sperm:
   a. No production
   b. Reduced production
   c. Abnormal production
2. Problems with transport
   a. Blocked epididymis
   b. Blocked Vas Deferens
3. Problems with ejaculation
   a. Impotence
   b. Premature ejaculation
   c. Retrograde ejaculation

HOW LONG SHOULD WE WAIT BEFORE GETTING THIS LOOKED INTO?

If, after 18 months of sexual intercourse without contraception, there has not been a pregnancy.

If the female partner is over 35 years of age, earlier investigation (after 12 months) is advisable. Both partners should attend the doctor together, preferably by appointment.

WHAT WILL THE DOCTOR DO?

The doctor will ask you both questions and will examine both of you. Likely points of discussion:

Your partner's menstrual cycle

If you have you fathered children in a previous relationship

If you had mumps after puberty.

These can cause a problem with sperm production in the testes. The testes will have been sore and tender at that time

If you ever had an injury to the groin or surgery in the groin area ie hernia repair or undescended testicle operation

General fitness questions

Any history of sexually transmitted disease

Medication you may be on

How often you are having sexual intercourse - 3 or 4 times a week is suggested for couples having difficulty in conceiving.

Timing of intercourse in relation to partner's monthly cycle

It is important that intercourse takes place around the time of egg production in the female. Your partner can easily be taught how to recognise this time. Increased sexual activity around the time of ovulation may well prove successful

Examination Male
1. Testes
a) Size - if very small there may be a hormonal problem.-.or they may have failed to develop
b) Varicocele - see chapter 5
c) Tenderness
   - mumps after puberty?

2. Epididymis - infection?
   Vas - the doctor should be able to feel.this on both sides

3. Penis

Following this your doctor may require a sample of semen fluid for a sperm count. This cannot be taken in a condom as there is a chemical in the condom that would kill the sperm. It must be brought to a laboratory within 2 hours of being taken. If your sperm count is low or abnormal the test should be repeated in a few months, as something transient may have affected it, i.e. a recent infection.

A repeat sperm count three months later may be normal.

FAILURE TO PRODUCE SPERM: (5% OF MALE INFERTILITY)

Treatment:
1. Lack of hormones may be treated with medication by.mouth or by injection
2. Testes fails to respond to hormones - post injury, mumps etc.

There is no effective treatment. if there is no sperm.

For men with a persistently low sperm count, there have been recent developments which offer hope for the future. A new technique involves taking some of the man's sperm, and with a minuscule lance injecting the sperm into an individual egg. If successful, the fertilised egg is then transferred to the mother's womb. This has had a relatively low success rate of 17% as of yet. This is due to problems with the natural chemicals the sperm has at its tip to gain entry into the female cells. The chemicals interfere with the sperm binding with the egg and the researchers are now trying to develop a way of 'washing' the sperm before they are injected into the egg. In addition, the doctors feel that their use of this research may extend to the whole area of male infertility, as their understanding of all the processes involved in infertility improves.

BLOCKED TUBES

> Surgery may be considered but the results are very disappointing. No other effective treatment.

EJACULATION PROBLEMS:

> 1. Impotence - see chapter 7
> 2. Premature ejaculation - see chapter 7
> 3. Retrograde ejaculation - see chapter 7

The overall figures for treating male infertility are disappointing. 20% of males attending a male infertility clinic are eventually able to father a child. As noted above, researchers in the U.K. are very hopeful of major breakthroughs in male fertility in the next few years.

Chapter 7: Male Sexual Problems

WHAT IS A SEXUAL PROBLEM?

A sexual problem exists if a person or a person's partner has an unsatisfactory sex life and finds his/her sexual tensions unrelieved.

WHAT IS NORMAL?

Normal sexual behaviour is whatever suits you provided nobody else suffers. Normal sexual appetite shows a huge variation and can often be the source of tension within a relationship. Partners often need to compromise. Sexual activity does not end at thirty or forty, as many young people seem to think. With ageing, men may find arousal physically slower. It may take a little longer to get an erection and it also may take a little longer to reach a climax. It might likewise take a little longer to get another erection after ejaculating.

Sexual problems in males
ERECTION PROBLEMS
EJACULATION PROBLEMS
SEXUAL DRIVE PROBLEMS

ERECTION PROBLEMS

A man is said to have an erection problem if he has persistent difficulty in getting and/or maintaining an erection. It is common for most men to have difficulty with erections at some stage in their lives. This can be due to various reasons such as tiredness, illness, lack of interest or lack of stimulation.

Sometimes a particular stimulus can produce an erection but not another, i.e. oral sex but not vaginal sex. There may also be difficulties at the start of a sexual relationship, usually due to anxiety. Relaxing and arousing your partner and vice-versa without penetrative sexual intercourse (sensual mas-sage, hand stimulation, etc.) may well help to reduce worries about performance in this situation.

QUESTIONS YOU CAN ASK YOURSELF IF YOU HAVE DIFFICULTIES WITH ERECTION:

1. Do you have an erection on waking in the morning?
2. Do you get an erection with any sexual stimulus, for example, sexual images or masturbation?
3. Does having sexual intercourse worry you?
4. Are you on any medication?
5. Do you suffer from any illness?
6. Do you feel the desire for sexual intercourse?

Erection problems can occur for:

a) a psychological reason
b) a physical problem
c) a combination of both

Answers to these questions are often helpful in deciding which is the most likely cause:

DO YOU HAVE AN ERECTION IN THE MORNING?

If the answer is yes, it suggests the problem is more likely to be psychological. The physical ability is there but, for some reason, you are not getting sufficiently aroused to have an erection.

Tackling Men's Health

DO YOU GET AN ERECTION WITH ANY STIMULUS?

If you get an erection while, for instance, watching a sex scene on television but not with your regular partner, the problem is more likely to be psychological than physical.

DO YOU GET WORRIED ABOUT HAVING SEXUAL INTERCOURSE?

This not an uncommon problem. A lot of men become anxious about their sexual performance and the sexual expectations of their partner. A lot of this is due to lack of communication between partners and an undue haste to have full penetrative sex.

ARE YOU TAKING ANY MEDICATION?

Certain drugs may cause impotence (an ability to have or maintain an erection). For example:
1. Alcohol
2. Cannabis

Some members of these drug families:
3. Anti-blood pressure tablets
4. Anti-depressants
5. Anxiolytic drugs - anti-anxiety
6. Diuretics - 'fluid' tablets
7. Anti-ulcer drugs

This is not a complete list so consult your doctor if you are taking any medications.

ARE YOU SUFFERING FROM ANY ILLNESS?

Some illnesses cause impotence. These are usually long-term illnesses. They usually affect either the nerves to the penis, for instance spinal injury or multiple sclerosis, or the blood vessels that supply the penis, for instance peripheral vascular disease [blockage of arteries]. The most common definite physical cause found is diabetes, which involves a combination of both nerve and blood vessel malfunction.

DO YOU FEEL THE DESIRE FOR SEXUAL INTERCOURSE?

If the answer is no, then there may be a physical cause, but more often it is due to non-physical causes. This is discussed later under low sex drive.

HOW DO I DEAL WITH THE PROBLEM IF THE CAUSE IS PSYCHOLOGICAL?

Consult your doctor. He will firstly try to outrule any contribution from a physical cause. He may suggest a consultation with both you and your partner, if you have one. He may suggest a series of measures which you could both undertake to try to solve the problem, or he may feel you require special help from a sex counsellor. These are usually psychologists with an expertise in sexual difficulties. One of the saddest things a GP can hear is that a couple he has been seeing as patients have had sexual problems for a long time, but have been too embarrassed to talk to their doctor about it.

The rate of success for couples who seek help is high.

WHAT TREATMENT WILL I GET FOR MY IMPOTENCE IF THE PROBLEM IS PSYCHOLOGICAL?

There is no drug treatment. If you are seen by a sex counsellor, he will usually see you together as a couple. He will, hopefully, be able to get both of you to talk about the problems. Often this alone may help a lot as many couples do not talk to each other about their sexual needs, what arouses them, their worries regarding performance etc.

He or your doctor may suggest a period of abstinence from full penetrative sex for, for instance, two months. In this time you and your partner may be asked to try different techniques of arousal. Initially you both may be asked to massage each other without touching the breasts, genital or bottom area. You are asked to focus on the enjoyment of being massaged or of being the masseur/masseuse.

If you felt you were getting satisfaction after a period of days, you would be allowed to move on to the next phase. This involves massage of the whole body including the breasts, genitals and anal area. It is important to stress that it is not massage of just those areas but of the whole body. Once you feel relaxed and are enjoying this sexual arousal, you can usually go on to full intercourse again.

IF MY PROBLEM IS MEDICATION-RELATED, WHAT SHOULD I DO?

Firstly, discuss it with your doctor, as an alternative form of medication may be needed. Then give up the medication that may be causing the problem. This is successful in most cases. Where it fails, some form of prosthesis may be considered (see below).

IF MY PROBLEM IS PHYSICAL THEN WHAT SHOULD I DO?

Only in some cases is drug treatment the answer. Other treatments are available. These include

1. Surgery with insertion of a prosthesis.

   A prosthesis is a device inserted at operation which may allow a man suffering from impotence to have and maintain an erection. One type is made of a flexible rod, which gives a permanent erection. As it is flexible, the rod can be adjusted so as not to be noticed under clothing.

   Another involves a pump mechanism, which can inflate the penis when necessary. This involves a balloon type pump inserted in the scrotum which inflates the penis

2. Injection.

   The penis can be made erect by injection of a drug which will create an erection. The erection will usually last for 60 to 90 minutes.

   With these methods a man is usually able to enjoy normal sexual activity and achieve orgasm.

2. EJACULATION PROBLEMS

PREMATURE EJACULATION

This is a condition where a man ejaculates too quickly, that is before he and his partner are sufficiently aroused to achieve sexual satisfaction from intercourse. It is not uncommon for a man to experience premature ejaculation on one or more occasion, but where it is on-going it can be a problem. This is not a particularly common problem, but where it exists it can cause sexual frustration for both partners. It also increases anxiety in the male regarding 'performance', which tends to make the problem worse.

Premature ejaculation is common when sexual intercourse takes place for the first time or when it takes place with a new partner. This is usually self-correcting as the anxiety decreases and the man gets more experienced, learning how to control his ejaculation. Use of a condom reduces penis sensitivity and may thereby slow down the ejaculation. Anxiety is the root cause of most cases. This is often based on a lack of communication between sexual partners which leads to a misunderstanding of each other's expectations from sexual intercourse and anxiety about performance.

WHAT IS THE TREATMENT FOR PREMATURE EJACULATION?

a) Reducing sexual anxiety - the couple should practise the technique described under the treatment for impotence. This involves abstinence from full penetrative intercourse and re-focusing on the sensual pleasures of mutual stimulation.

b) Seeing a sex counsellor.

c) The squeeze technique. This involves you and your partner learning the sensations that you experience before you ejaculate. At the moment you feel like ejaculating your partner can delay your ejaculation by squeezing the penis just below the glans, which prevents ejaculation. This technique is complex and is best undertaken when both you and your partner have been instructed in how to carry it out correctly.

DELAYED EJACULATION OR FAILURE TO EJACULATE

This is a rare complaint. With ageing it is not uncommon to experience occasional occurrences of delayed ejaculation or failure to ejaculate.

QUESTIONS REGARDING DELAYED EJACULATION/FAILURE TO EJACULATE:

    a) Are you taking any medication?

        Some drugs may cause delayed ejaculation. Consult your doctor if you are on any medication.

    b) Are you anxious regarding intercourse?

        As discussed under both impotence and premature ejaculation, anxiety regarding performance can be a source of sexual problems. Open discussion between the two partners is often helpful. Sometimes the contribution of a doctor or sex counsellor in these discussions can be helpful as couples can, for various reasons, have difficulty talking about sexual matters openly and frankly.

        The technique described under the treatment of impotence where the couple abstain from intercourse and re-focus on their mutual arousal without full intercourse can he very helpful.

    c) Are you, or have you been, practising the 'withdrawal' method of contraception?

        This involves the man withdrawing his penis before ejaculating. If this is practised over a long period of time, then it may be difficult to stop the habit and you find you cannot ejaculate without withdrawing. This may be a transient problem. If it persists consult your doctor.

    d) Are you able to ejaculate when stimulated by a method other than penetrative sexual intercourse? If for instance, you can ejaculate when masturbating the problem is likely to be one of sexual anxiety (see under b above)

Sex drive problems

Sex drive varies from man to man, and for each individual man from time to time. It is also affected by outside influences such as stress, depression, physical illness, alcohol or medication. It may also be affected by anxiety regarding performance or by difficulties within a relationship.

Some men have always had a low sex drive and this may not be a problem within a relationship, particularly if discussed openly with his partner. If not discussed, the lack of sexual contact may be misinterpreted as lack of love or affection. However, in some relationships the sexual drive of the partner may be much higher and this may lead to tension in a relationship. If this is happening, it is probably best to discuss this together with your doctor. If you have noticed a sudden change in your sex drive there are questions you can ask yourself:

1. Have I had a physical illness recently?
2. Have I started any medication recently?
3. Have I been drinking more alcohol recently?
4. Have I been under pressure recently?
5. Have I been excessively tired recently?
6. Have I had any sexual problems recently?
7. How is my relationship with my partner?

1. PHYSICAL ILLNESS

It is not uncommon for sex drive to be reduced for a period following illness. Prolonged periods of reduced sex drive is common following certain illnesses like hepatitis and infectious mononucleosis (glandular fever), and from any on-going medical condition like rheumatoid arthritis

2. MEDICATION.

Discuss your medication with your GP. Certain drugs may reduce your sex drive. However, it may be the condition for which you are being treated that is responsible.

3. ALCOHOL

Increased alcohol consumption on a regular basis does not 'increase the desire'. It reduces the desire and 'reduces the performance'. It may even lead to erection problems.

4. PRESSURE

Stress is one of the commonest causes of reduced or absent sex drive. It can cause problems in a relationship unless discussed openly with your partner. Having intercourse just to live up to your perceived 'duties' is not a very good idea as it may lead to anxiety about performance. Dealing with the stress is the solution.

5. OVERTIRED

This may be a symptom of stress or physical disease. It is better to deal with the underlying problem first. If the problem is physical, then ensure that you have adequate rest before you attempt sexual intercourse again. Discuss this with your partner, as it may be misinterpreted as lack of affection, if unexplained. Trying to have intercourse when you are tired is likely to lead to sex that is unsatisfactory for both of you. This is likely to be interpreted by your partner as disinterest and can cause difficulties in your relationship. It is better to he honest about how you feel.

6. SEXUAL PROBLEM

If you have developed another sexual problem, such as erection difficulties, you may lose interest

7. RELATIONSHIP

in sex. This may be due to anxiety regarding your ability to 'perform'. Treatment of the underlying problem (see above) should improve your sex drive.

If there are problems, either sexual or non-sexual, between you and your partner, it may result in a reduction in your sex drive. If there are major differences of a non-sexual nature between you and your partner, your sexual relationship must invariably suffer. You may find your interest in sex disappears as a result.

Your reduced sex drive may not just be with your partner but with all thought of sexual activity. This problem cannot, in general, be solved without first solving the problem within the relationship. A sexual problem between you and your partner may produce a reduction in sex drive. This is often because the couple are unable to discuss the problem openly. Statements such as 'I'm not interested in sex anyway' are made to prevent hurting a partner's feelings. Whether this is true or not, it can become the accepted fact within the relationship.

It can be easier for the couple to agree that they are not having intercourse because 'neither of us are very interested' than for the couple or the individual to work on solving the problem. Frank and open discussion about sexual matters may not be possible for them without an outsider, such as a sex counsellor. It is taking the first step - admitting there is a problem - that is often the most difficult. Once the couple have got that far, the next step, seeking help, is not as difficult. In general practise, it is not uncommon to hear of couples who have been married for several years without having had sexual intercourse. Once they seek help, almost all of these couples end up with a sexually satisfying relationship.

Chapter 8: Contraception.

This chapter aims to give men a good understanding of the available methods of contraception and a brief guide to female contraception.

The effectiveness of a contraceptive is measured in the number of pregnancies occurring in a hundred women years. This is measured in units of one hundred women who become pregnant while using a particular method of contraception for one year. During the rest of this chapter the percentage sign % will be used to signify this rate.

Number of pregnancies per 100/Women Years

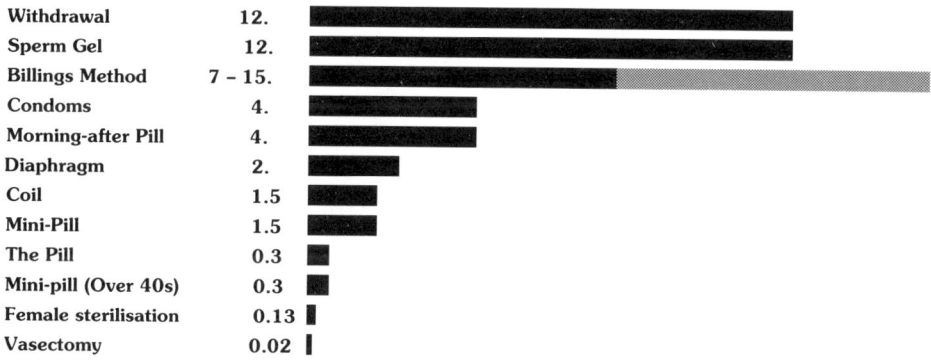

Withdrawal	12.
Sperm Gel	12.
Billings Method	7 - 15.
Condoms	4.
Morning-after Pill	4.
Diaphragm	2.
Coil	1.5
Mini-Pill	1.5
The Pill	0.3
Mini-pill (Over 40s)	0.3
Female sterilisation	0.13
Vasectomy	0.02

For a man there are only two effective methods of contraception which are dealt with later in this chapter:

1. CONDOM
2. VASECTOMY

Other methods of male contraception:
WITHDRAWAL METHOD

Failure rate: 12%

This is not an effective form of contraception. Once the penis is erect there may be sperm present at the top of the penis. Sperm may therefore enter the female vagina after penetration but before ejaculation. Withdrawal before ejaculation is too late. There are other **problems** with this method:

Timing of withdrawal, lack of satisfaction for one or both partners, difficulty with delayed ejaculation. After using this method for a prolonged period, the man may become unable to ejaculate while in the female vagina.

SPERMICIDAL CREAM/GEL.

Failure rate: 12%

This is not an effective contraceptive on its own. The one area where spermicidal creams are occasionally used on their own is by women who are around the menopause and who have not used, or have difficulty using, other methods (condoms). Its use is mainly as an additional protection with the barrier methods of contraception. (Barrier methods are those which block sperm getting into the womb. e.g. condoms for the male or diaphragm for the female). In addition, some spermicidal gels have been shown to have an anti-HIV effect, in particular Nonoxynol 9. For those involved in regular 'casual sex' it is important to check that the spermicidal gel on their condom is nonoxynol

CONDOMS/SHEATH/DUREX'

Failure Rate: 4%

The condom is a sheath which is applied to the erect penis. Over the centuries they have been made from various materials, but the modern condoms are made from latex rubber. This gives the necessary contraceptive effect without huge loss of sensitivity. They act by preventing the entry of the sperm into the female. The most common reason for failure is the condom bursting. Manufacturers admit a one in twenty chances of this happening. An American study found four out of five couples experienced a condom breakage over a period of 18 months. The thinner the condom the more likely this is to happen. The condom can also be damaged while being applied.

Advantages of condoms:
1. Reasonably effective
2. Give protection against sexually transmitted diseases
3. No side-effects (except local allergy).

Disadvantages of condoms:
1. Not as effective as other methods (diaphragm, Pill)
2. Reduced sexual enjoyment for either/both partner due to decreased penile sensitivity in the male or decreased sexual arousal in the female.
3. Allergy to rubber - either partner may have or develop an allergy to rubber. The majority of times that condoms fail as a contraceptive is due to some failure in technique of applying or removing them, or a condom bursting. This is much less likely to occur if the following rules are followed:

a) The condom should be in good condition. If the foil wrapping is broken, they should not be used

b) Use a condom pre-coated with a spermicidal gel or use a spermicidal gel with a condom. The preference would be for Nonoxynol 9 as it has some protection against the HIV (AIDS) virus.

c) The stronger the condom, the better the protection. The thinner condoms improve penis sensitivity but are more likely to burst.

d) The air should be removed from the teat of the condom before applying it to the penis. It is more likely to burst if this is not done.

e) The condom should be applied to the erect penis before there is any contact with the vagina. (The erect penis may have sperm at its tip which may be transported to the entrance of the vagina to the womb without full penetration taking place).

f) Care should be taken when applying the condom. Fingernails, jewellery or other objects may tear it.

g) Lubrication - it is important that there is adequate lubrication. Foreplay and the spermicidal gel normally achieve this. Don't use other oils as these appear to have an eroding effect on the condom. Manufacturers have found that oils as varied as baby oil, suntan lotion to cooking oils are implicated in some condom breakage.

h) Take care when removing the penis from the vagina to hold the base of the condom to ensure its safe withdrawal.

i) Do not re-use the condom if further intercourse is planned. Remove the first condom and carefully apply the new one.

Tackling Men's Health

VASECTOMY - MALE STERILISATION

Failure rate: 0.02%

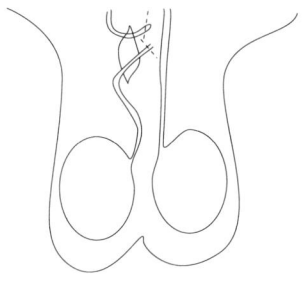

Vasectomy is a permanent solution to male contraception. The operation involves the division of the vas deferens, the tube that carries the sperm from the testes. As there is a vas deferens on both the left and right sides, the operation is done on both sides. It should only be undergone by someone who has thought through the consequences and is certain he does not want further children now or in the future. It is not a solution to sexual problems within the marriage. It is rarely performed on males under thirty years of age.

In general before being considered for vasectomy, you will be counselled regarding your decision, the operation and its side effects. This is usually done with both you and your partner present.

QUESTIONS YOU WILL BE ASKED:

1. Are you certain your family is complete?
2. Have you considered how you would feel if one of your children died?
3. Have you considered what would happen if your spouse died and you had a new partner and your new partner wanted a child?

Having discussed these questions with you, your doctor will then examine you to check your scrotum (see below)

DO I HAVE TO STAY IN HOSPITAL TO HAVE A VASECTOMY?

Most men have the operation done as an outpatient under local anaesthetic in a family planning clinic, GP's surgery, or hospital Outpatients Clinic. However, it is safer for some men to have the procedure done in hospital as an outpatient under general anaesthetic. The reasons for this being necessary can be divided into

1. Problems in the groin or scrotum area.
2 General medical problems

1. Problems in the groin area
    a) If the vas deferens is not easily felt
    b) If you have a hernia or previously had one repaired
    c) If you have a varicocele see Chapter 5
    d) If you have a large hydrocele - see Chapter 5
    e) If you have an infection of the genital tract.

2. General Medical Problems
    a) If you have had a recent heart attack or suffer from heart disease.
    b) If you suffer from diabetes
    c) If you are on anti-coagulant (blood thinning) medication (ie Warfarin)
    d) If you have had a bad reaction to local anaesthetic in the past.

It must be emphasised that the vast majority of men have the operation under local anaesthetic.

THE OPERATION

The doctor locates the cord in your scrotum. He injects local anaesthetic into the skin around the vas deferens (the spermatic cord). This can cause slight discomfort for a few seconds. Once the local anaesthetic has worked you do not feel any more.

The doctor then makes a small cut of about a centimetre in the skin and brings out the cord (vas). He divides it and takes a one centimetre piece out of it. He then ties both cut ends separately or uses a fine probe to burn them. This is to stop both ends joining up again. The skin is then closed with one or two stitches. The stitches are absorbable so they dissolve after 7 to 14 days

CAN I GO BACK TO WORK AFTER THE OPERATION?

No. You are advised to rest from physical activity for 2 days. If your job is physically intensive a longer period of rest may be recommended.

WHAT PROBLEMS MIGHT I HAVE IN THE FIRST FEW DAYS AFTER THE VASECTOMY?

Most men have little or no problems. Those that do arise are:

1. Pain - usually mild discomfort relieved by paracetemol. It is better not to take aspirin for the pain as it may cause a little bleeding.
2. Bleeding - there is usually a small amount of bruising after the vasectomy. Sometimes there may be more. If this happens consult your doctor. Usually rest is sufficient treatment.
3. Infection - occasionally mild infection may occur in the scrotum. Consult your doctor. The treatment is rest and anti-biotics

AM I STERILE AFTER THE OPERATION?

No. There are still sperm in the tubes above where the vas was divided. These have to be ejaculated before you become sterile. This usually takes three to four months. This will be checked at about four months with two sperm counts. A sample of the semen ejaculated at 16 and 18 weeks after the vasectomy is taken. If two samples in a row are free of sperm you will be told you are sterile. Until then, another form of contraception should be used.

HOW SOON CAN I RESUME SEXUAL INTERCOURSE?

This depends on the degree of discomfort after the operation, but is usually one or two weeks. As already mentioned you must use another method of contraception until you are told by the doctor that you are sterile.

IS THE OPERATION ALWAYS SUCCESSFUL?

No. There is a failure rate. In less than 1 in 200 men the vas or tube reconnects. Most of these cases arise in the first few months after the operation and are usually picked up by the sperm count.

WILL THE OPERATION AFFECT MY VIRILITY?

No. The operation does not affect your sex drive or physical satisfaction. You will still get an ejaculation at orgasm, but it will not contain any sperm.

ARE THERE ANY LONG-TERM COMPLICATIONS OF VASECTOMY?

1 Pain - it is not.usual to have on-going discomfort after vasectomy, but there have been some cases of on-going pain.

2 Recanalisation - very rare - after the first few months the vas can re-form and the man can become fertile again.

In addition, there is a question about an increased rate of testicular cancer and prostatic cancer following vasectomy. With testicular cancer - one trial showed an increased incidence of testicular cancer in long term follow-up of men after vasectomy.

However, other trials have failed to show this. At present it is unproven that vasectomy increases the incidence of testicular cancer.

With prostate cancer it is also unproven. Further research is taking place.

CAN THE OPERATION BE REVERSED?

Yes. The success of reversal, ie fertility, is not high. It is most likely to be successful shortly after the vasectomy and becomes increasingly unlikely to be successful with time. The reality is that if you are thinking of having a vasectomy you should consider it to be irreversible.

BRIEF GUIDE TO FEMALE CONTRACEPTION
BILLINGS/'SAFE PERIOD' METHOD/NATURAL FAMILY PLANNING

This involves the woman recognising when she is producing an egg. She does this by taking her temperature daily and by recognising the changes in her vaginal mucous. There is no intercourse before the egg is produced and for two days after it is produced ie approximately the first 17 days of the menstrual cycle.

Failure rate 7-15% with careful use

Advantages
1. The only method allowed by the Roman Catholic Church
2. Natural. No side effects. No interference with normal cycle.

Disadvantages
1. High failure rate
2. Requires abstinence from intercourse for a lot of the monthly cycle.

THE PILL - COMBINED ORAL CONTRACEPTION

This is a combination of two hormones and works by stopping the woman producing an egg. It is exceptionally safe in non smokers. They can use the.pill.until 45 years old. Smokers have to stop using the pill when 35.

Failure rate 0.3%

Advantages

1. Highly effective. The most effective form of reversible contraception
2. Easily taken
3. Protective against certain cancers -cancer of the ovary and womb.

Disadvantages

1. Side effects. Some women cannot tolerate the pill for various reasons. Examples of this are mood changes, headaches, weight gain. Occasionally there may be blood clotting problems, particularly in smokers
2. May not be effective:
a) With vomiting or diahorroea -the pill may be vomited up or rushed through without being absorbed in the stomach.
b) If taking certain medicines for instance certain antibiotics, some anti epilepsy drugs
3. Possible increase in breast cancer rate. This is considered to be slight and less likely with the newer generation of pills. Overall the pill is protective against cancer.

THE MINI PILL

This just contains one hormone which works in two ways.

1. It causes changes in the neck of the womb that prevents the sperm getting into the womb.
2. Prevents the lining of the womb from allowing the egg to be implanted.

Failure rate 1.5% (.3% in over 40s)

Advantages
1. Particularly effective for women over 40. As effective as the pill for a 25 year old
2. Can be taken when breast feeding
3. Can continue taking it to any age.
4. Less side effects than the pill

Disadvantages
1. Must be taken at the same time every day
2. Can be interfered with by vomiting, diarrhoea or medication
3. Side effects – in particular problems with bleeding and the monthly cycle.

THE COIL - INTRAUTERINE CONTRACEPTIVE DEVICE

This is a device which is put into the womb by a doctor. It acts by preventing the fertilised egg from sticking onto the wall of the womb.

Failure rate 1.5%

Advantages
1. Can easily be left in up to five years.
2. The woman can check it is still there as there is a little thread attached to the coil which she can feel in the vagina.

Disadvantages
1. May not be suitable for women who have not had a child.
2. She may experience heavier monthly periods.
3. Occasionally infection may occur in the pelvis.

4. Increased occurrence of ectopic pregnancy, that is pregnancy outside the womb.

THE DIAPHRAGM/CAP

This is put over the neck of the womb by the woman before intercourse. It is used with a spermicidal gel or cream. It prevents sperm getting into the womb.

Failure Rate 2%

Advantages

1. Effective and easy to use once taught how

Disadvantage

1. Allergy to rubber occasionally
2. Some women find an increase in the occurrence of urinary tract infections.

POST COITAL CONTRACEPTION. MORNING AFTER PILL

The morning after pill is for use after

a) Unprotected intercourse

b) Failed barrier method ie burst condom

It acts by preventing the fertilised egg being implanted in the womb

Failure rate 1 - 4% depending on proximity of intercourse to egg formation.

While called the Morning After Pill it can be effective up to 72 hours after intercourse. It should not be used as a regular method of contraception, as the dosage of hormones is very high

FEMALE STERILISATION

Failure rate 0.13%

Tubal ligation is the cutting or clipping of the fallopian tubes, thereby stopping the delivery of the eggs from the ovary to the womb. It requires a general (full) anaesthetic.

Occasional failures occur,

It is reversible but success after reversal is low.

Chapter 9: Sexually-transmitted diseases - STDs

The incidence of sexually-transmitted diseases in on the increase. This is due to two factors : firstly, the increase in the number of sexual contacts and secondly, more extensive travel abroad. Casual sex in certain areas of the world carries a high likelihood of infection with a sexually transmitted disease. The infected travellers may return without being aware of being infected, and may allow the infection to spread through further sexual activity on their return. In addition, the infections that are brought back from these hot spots of STDs may be a strain of infection that has become resistant to the standard treatments used here.

HOW DO I AVOID SEXUALLY-TRANSMITTED DISEASE?

1. Monogamy. Living with one partner who is only having sexual intercourse with you.
2. 'Safe sex'.
a) Limit the number of sexual partners
b) Have sex only with someone you know not to be infected.
c) Use a condom if having vaginal or anal intercourse.

'Safe Sex' should really be called 'Safer Sex' as once you have more than one sexual partner, you increase your chances of contracting a sexually-transmitted disease. Also, while your partners may say they are free of infection, 30-40% of females with gonorrhoea have no symptoms, and a large percentage of people who are HIV positive (i.e. carrying the AIDS virus) may be unaware they are infective. Finally, condoms do not give complete protection as, for instance, they may burst during intercourse.

WHAT SYMPTOMS SHOULD I LOOK FOR?
1. Painful urination
2. Discharge from penis.
3. Itchy penis
4. Sore, lump, blister or ulcer on the penis
These may be painful or painless.

1. PAINFUL URINATION MAY BE DUE TO:
   a) A kidney tract infection which is not sexually transmitted.
   b) Gonorrhoea
   c) Non-specific Urethritis
2. DISCHARGE FROM THE PENIS MAY BE DUE TO:
   a) Gonorrhoea - Usually a pus discharge
   b) Non-specific Urethritis - usually a clear discharge earlier on, becoming thicker if left untreated.
3. ITCHY PENIS
   a) Non-specific Urethritis - sometimes this is only felt early in the morning at the bottom of the penis.
   b) Herpes genitalis - the first symptom is an itchy feeling on the shaft of the penis, which is followed by small fluid-filled blisters which are painful.
   c) Candida (Thrush). It is difficult to call Candida a sexually-transmitted disease, as it occurs in three-quarters of all females. It occurs without sexual transmission in the female, but the male then gets penile thrush from sexual contact with his partner.

Tackling Men's Health

The male should apply anti-fungal cream if his partner is being treated for thrush even if he has no symptoms. Candida in the male usually produces a cream-coloured thick coating on the glans (top of penis), under the foreskin. This coating can be wiped away easily with a cloth. Underneath this covering the glans is redder than usual. Treatment is with a cream. Your partner may also need treatment.

4. SORES, LUMPS, BLISTERS AND ULCERS.
   a) Syphilis
   A painless sore on the penis is characteristic of the early stage of syphilis. It is highly infectious.
   b) Herpes genitalis
   After an itchy penis for a day or so, a crop of blisters develops. These burst, then a day or so later small red and wet ulcers appear.
   c) Anogenital warts
   Usually, but not always, sexually-transmitted. See your own doctor or go to an STD clinic. Do not try to treat them yourself.

If you feel you have a sexually-transmitted disease see your doctor or go to your local STD clinic. You need treatment, but also you need to be screened for the other sexually-transmitted diseases, which may be present but producing no symptoms.

Common sexually-transmitted diseases:

Gonorrhea

HOW LONG AFTER SEXUAL INTERCOURSE WOULD I GET THESE SYMPTOMS?

2 to 10 days.

WHAT ARE THE SYMPTOMS?

1. Painful urination
2. Pus-like discharge from the penis

HOW IS IT DIAGNOSED?

1. Sample of pus examined in a laboratory

HOW IS IT TREATED?

Antibiotics, either by mouth or injection

WHAT HAPPENS IF I DON'T GET IT TREATED?

1. Blockage of the urethra - difficulty passing urine
2. Blockage of vas or epididymis leading to sterility
3. Spread of infection.

Non-specific Urethritis

HOW LONG AFTER SEXUAL CONTACT WILL I GET SYMPTOMS?

6 to 48 days

WHAT ARE THE SYMPTOMS?

1. Discomfort or tingling at the bottom of the penis
2. Symptoms only present, or worse, in the early morning
3. Discharge - initially clear and in small quantity, becoming thicker and more copious if left untreated.

WHAT CAUSES IT?

Usually a bug called chlamydia.

WHAT IS THE TREATMENT?

    Antibiotics

Herpes genitalis

HOW LONG AFTER INTERCOURSE WILL I GET SYMPTOMS?

    Less than a week

WHAT ARE THE SYMPTOMS?

    You may have a flu-like illness with a raised temperature and headache.

    Local symptoms are

    1. Itchy penis followed by

    2. Blisters on the penis and sometimes on the thigh followed by

    3. Red, wet painful ulcers after the blisters burst

WHAT IS THE TREATMENT?

    Anti-viral cream or tablets

WILL THEY CURE IT?

    No, they will relieve the severe pain, but like their near relatives, cold sores, they recur. They remain dormant in your body until the conditions are right for recurrence. Recurrence of the herpes can be lessened by:

    1. General fitness.- don't get run down

    2. Ensure adequate lubrication before intercourse

    3. Use loose cotton underclothes

    4. Don't use bubble baths or perfumed soaps

    5. Avoid letting sunlight near the affected areas.

IF THEY ARE NOT CURED, CAN I INFECT A SEXUAL PARTNER AT ANY TIME?

    No. They are infective only at the blister or ulcer stage. Avoid intercourse, either oral or genital, at this stage. Using a condom reduces the risk of giving someone else the virus but is not to be relied upon at this stage.

Avoid touching the sores unless treating them. Wash your hands after touching the sores.and have a towel/cloth for your use only.

Syphilis

HOW LONG AFTER INTERCOURSE BEFORE IT APPEARS?

Two to four weeks generally, but may occur any time from 9-90 days

SYMPTOMS

First stage

Painless hard ulcer on the penis (or anus in homosexuals). This usually heals within three to ten weeks.

Second stage

Two months later general symptoms appear

1. Temperature
2. Joint pains
3. Feeling unwell
4. Sore throat.

Skin: red/brown with non itchy lumps

Groin and underarms: warty growths

Mouth or penis: "Snail-track" ulcers- a continuous line of ulceration.

Third stage

If untreated during the first two stages, then the disease may progress to this stage which can produce marked brain, heart, bone and/or skin complications.

Not many people in the developed world nowadays reach stage 3 of syphilis due to the wider availability of treatment.

WHAT IS THE TREATMENT?

Injection of antibiotics over a period of days

Anogenital warts

As mentioned above, these are not necessarily sexually- transmitted. However, in those people who feel they have got them through sexual contact it is important:

A) TO BE SCREENED FOR OTHER STDS
B) NOT TO TREAT THEM YOURSELF

WHAT IS THE TREATMENT?

Usually a paint or cream is applied at the clinic.

Hepatitis B

USUALLY TRANSMITTED BY:

1. Sexual intercourse
2. Blood products - contact with blood products through transfusion, used needles, etc.,

WHAT ARE THE SYMPTOMS?

1. Jaundice - dark skin, yellow whites of eyes, dark urine, pale bowel motion.
2. Marked tiredness
3. Nausea
4. Lack of interest in food or smoking

TREATMENT:

Rest and limited diet, free of fat and alcohol. A hospital stay may be necessary.

CAN IT BE PREVENTED?

Yes. There is an effective vaccine available for those in regular contact with blood products, i.e., doctors, dentists, nurses, lab technicians etc.; it is also available to people such as policemen and prison officers who are most at risk from attack by people like drug users who may be infected with Hepatitis B.

Acquired Immuno deficiency Syndrome AIDS

WHAT IS AIDS?

Aids is a condition in which the body's ability to defend itself is damaged. This allows infections that the body can normally deal with to flourish. It also allows cancers that are normally rare to occur.

WHAT CAUSES AIDS?

A virus called HIV is thought to be the cause.

HOW DO I GET HIV?

1. Sexual intercourse
2. Contact with infected blood or blood products
3. Used needles.

WHO IS MOST LIKELY TO GET HIV?

1. Homosexuals
2. Bisexuals
3. Drug abusers who share needles
4. Female partners of AIDS patients
5. Babies of female AIDS patients

This picture is changing however, with more heterosexual HIV positive people in the sexually active population.

WHAT ARE THE SYMPTOMS?

Early Phase (within months of infection)

a) no symptoms
b) flu-like illness for 1-2 weeks - tiredness, joint/muscle pains, above normal temperature,

sore throat, lymph gland swelling.

Although symptoms are slight or absent at this point the person can be HIV positive and capable of infecting others. This is what makes it difficult to prevent the spread of AIDS.

Between 50 and 70% of people affected by the HIV virus go on to develop the later symptoms (Full-Blown AIDS).

Later symptoms:
1. Skin rashes
2. On-going weight loss/lack of energy
3. Unusual lung infections
4. Rare cancers

At this stage there is usually rapid disimprovement.

TREATMENT

There is no cure available at present. Treatment is currently aimed at the time between the early and late phases. During this time a blood test can be done to measure the defences which HIV attacks. If the defences are disimproving then treatment with drugs starts. In recent months further hopes have been raised that a vaccine for HIV is closer to being discovered.

For treatment and further information on sexually transmitted diseases contact your nearest STD clinic. Your local health board or GP will advise you on the nearest one to you.

Chapter 10: Work related disease and injury

Both men and women's health can be intimately connected with occupation. Certain occupations carry with them both an increased risk of disease directly associated with their work and an increased mortality (death) rate.

The greater mortality rate in some of these occupations is obvious i.e. labouring, fishermen, etc. Others are less obvious, e.g. publican (alcohol abuse and passive smoking), and some others are inexplicable, i.e. watchmakers/repairers.

The leading work-related diseases and injuries

1 Skin conditions
dermatitis, burns

2 Muscle/ligament/joint problems
back injury, neck injury, limb injury.

3. Occupational lung diseases
asbestos lung disease
silicon lung disease
coal miner's disease
occupational asthma
lung cancer

4. Accidental
accidental death
fractures
eye injuries

5. Toxic disorders
-either due to short exposure to something poisonous or a gradual build-up of a toxin due to repeated contact at work.

6. Psychological disorders
stress-related ill-health

personality problems
alcohol/drug problems
7. Occupational cancers
skin cancer
bladder cancer
leukaemia

This chapter aims to deal with the two major causes of loss of workdays: Dermatitis.and back pain

Dermatitis.

This is an irritation or inflammation of the skin. In the early stage the skin becomes red and itchy, and there may be blistering. If there are repeated episodes, the skin becomes hardened and there may be thickening of the skin with associated cracking. The most common cause of dermatitis is exposure to chemicals.

Dermatitis is responsible for more than half the work-related diseases in this country. The consequences for the person with contact dermatitis can be disastrous, as they may not be able to continue in their employment. The undamaged skin is an excellent protector of the body. It has a thick outside layer onto which it puts an oily substance which gives further protection. The skin is more prone to injury where:

1. The outer layer is thinner - eyelids, armpits, groin
2. There is a graze or cut
3. The oily covering is removed - by excessive hand-washing or use of solvents

Chemicals can produce dermatitis in two ways:
1. Direct irritation, e.g. acid
2. By producing an allergic reaction, e.g. cement

IRRITANT DERMATITIS

The severity of the irritation depends on
1. The dose or concentration of the chemical
2. The length of time it is in contact with the skin.

Therefore reduction of the concentration or contact time may prevent the irritation. Irritant dermatitis occurs on the area of skin where there has been contact with the skin.

                Groups of chemicals which may cause irritation
                        1. Alkalis
                        2. Acids
                        3. Metals
                        4. Solvents

ALLERGIC DERMATITIS

The chemicals pass through the outer layer of skin and produce a reaction in the body. This may not happen the first time there is contact with the chemical. In fact it may not happen until there has been on-going contact with the chemical for years. However, once the body has reacted to the chemical, future contact with it will produce a dermatitis. Unlike the contact dermatitis, the reaction may occur after dealing with tiny amounts of the chemical. Therefore the consequences of allergic dermatitis in relation to continuation of work are obvious.

The skin reaction does not always occur in the skin area with which the chemical has been in contact on that occasion. It may produce a reaction in a different area that has been previously sensitised. If, for instance, you have nickel allergy, and previously reacted to a neck-chain containing nickel, when your hands come into contact with nickel again you may develop a neck rash. This will happen where the skin was previously sensitised by the neck-chain, instead of a rash on the hands.

GROUPS OF CHEMICALS THAT MAY SENSITISE THE SKIN
1. Dyes
2. Some oils
3. Coal Tar
4. Resins
5. Insecticides
6. Photographic/printing chemicals

PREVENTION OF DERMATITIS

Employers have a major role in prevention of dermatitis by the provision of:.

1. Signs to indicate irritant chemicals: 'Irritant to Skin', 'Avoid Contact With Skin' 'Wear Gloves'.
2. Control procedures for contact with irritant substances, e.g. ventilation of solvents
3. Provision of proper washing facilities near workplace.

The employee must:

1. Be aware of irritant substances
2. Avoid contact where possible
3. Wear protective clothing where necessary i.e gloves - a cotton wool lining keeps skin dry from excess sweating
4. Maintain skin in good condition
a) clean skin properly, avoiding possible irritant soaps or cleansers. Detergent cleansers can often cause dermatitis
b) dry properly - clean towel
soft disposable towel
air-dryer with low-speed air-flow

c) apply hand-cream after every wash -it should be provided in every wash place.
5. Barrier creams appropriate to the chemical they are protecting against - non irritant.

These simple measures could prevent a possibly disabling condition. There is nothing complicated about them, and none of them are expensive.

Occupational Back Pain

Studies in Sweden have shown that about 70% of men suffer back pain during their active working years. The percentage of these injuries occurring in the workplace can be difficult to estimate as there can be financial advantages to saying your injury happened at work as distinct from a leisure activity. Where on-site medical services were provided, the incidence of work-related back pain was found to be lower than where medical services were not provided. A study in Great Britain found that 3.6% of all workdays lost were due to back pain.

Chronic back pain is the most common cause of reduced work capacity and decreased leisure time activity in the under 45 year olds.

TREATMENT OF BACK PAIN

This depends on the cause of the injury and the severity of the condition

Danger signs with back pain

1. Loss of, or difficulty with, bladder control
2. Loss of, or difficulty with, bowel control
3. Numbness or pins and needles in the saddle area (the area a saddle would be in contact with)
4. Difficulty with the power in both legs

Any one or more of these require urgent medical attention. Your doctor should be contacted immediately and you should move as little as possible. These symptoms suggest there is severe pressure on your spinal cord. This pressure may need to be removed surgically

Other symptoms which suggest that an early medical opinion is advisable:
1. Does the pain stop you from moving?
2. Does the pain shoot down the leg?
3. Is there weakness in one leg?
4. Is there numbness in one leg?

These symptoms suggest there may be a portion of the disc pressing on a nerve root in the back.

Most people with back pain do not experience these symptoms. Most back pain begins with an aching sensation in the back which commonly comes on, either suddenly - as after lifting something, or gradually - as after a day spent gardening or spent stooped whilst picking stones. In a lot of cases no definite cause for the pain starting can be found.

Treatment of this type of pain involves:

Resting by lying on the flat, preferably face-down. This should be followed by early, gentle mobilisation. In general, it is wise to avoid a sitting position, even at mealtimes. The physiotherapist may be of great benefit, not only in the treatment of the acute back pain, but also with advice regarding posture and avoiding future back problems. Most cases of back pain of this type will settle within a few weeks or occasionally months. While most people with back problems are anxious to have an x-ray of their backs, standard x-ray is seldom useful and is best left to the discretion of the doctor

RISK FACTORS FOR DEVELOPING BACK PAIN

1. Poor general fitness

   A comparison of people in the same job showed those who had been assessed as least fit were ten times more likely to develop back pain.

2. Smoking

   The cause is not clear. There are two theories:

a) repeated coughing putting extra strain on the disc

b) .smoking interfering with the supply of essential 'food' to the disc and surrounding areas

3. 'Heavy' lifting.

It is not just the weight of the article to be lifted that is of importance. The following must also be considered:

a) size/load too large

b) difficulty grasping the load

c) shifting the load

d) position of the load - if it has to be lifted at a distance from the body, or if the body is unstable while lifting, i e. does lifting involve rotation of the trunk?

4. Inadequate training for lifting
5. Unsuitable shoes or clothes for lifting

GENERAL MEASURES FOR PREVENTION OF BACK-ACHE.

Posture

Try to keep your head, trunk and legs in a straight line while standing or walking. No slouching.

Sitting

Keep your back straight; use a chair with a firm back and arm supports, which take additional strain off the back.

Correct sitting posture Incorrect sitting posture

Use a lectern to change the angle of your work

Sleeping: Incorrect

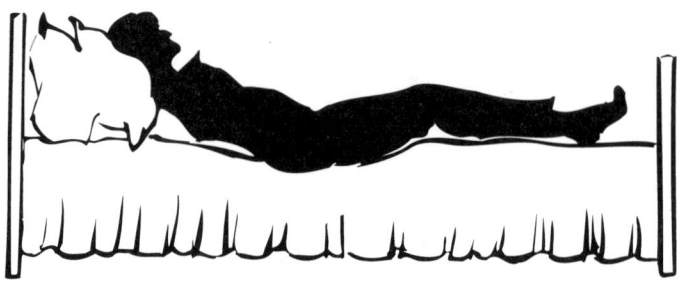

Correct: Use a firm mattress and one pillow. Place a cushion under the small of the back for extra support

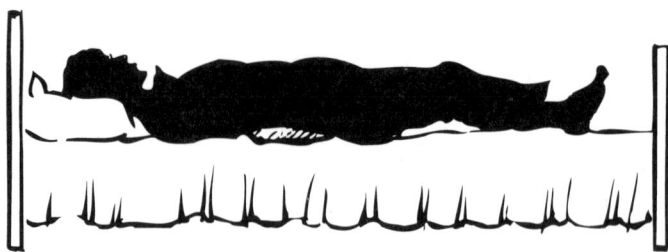

Lifting:
Bend your knees even if the load is already raised, e.g. boot of car;
keep your back straight.
These measures ensure the strain is taken on the big leg muscles at the front and back of the thigh

Chapter 11: Sports Injuries

This is not a specifically male area, but despite the recent upsurge in women taking part in sport, it is usually men that present at doctor's surgeries with sport-related injuries. There are three reasons for this:

> More men play sport.
> Men play more sports with physical contact.
> Men are more likely to play sport when unfit and more likely to use the wrong footwear/equipment.

Women who play sport seem to do so in a more structured way than their male counter-parts, with a gradual build-up to a higher level of performance. On the other hand, men of all ages seem to feel that they can immediately start playing as soon as they set eyes on a football/racquet/bat/club without giving a thought to their age or general fitness.

This chapter aims to give a guide to:

> PREVENTION OF SPORTS INJURIES
> GENERAL TREATMENT OF SPORTS INJURIES
> COMMON SPORTS INJURIES - HOW THEY HAPPEN AND THEIR TREATMENT.

This is not a comprehensive treatment of sports injuries, as it would take a complete book to deal adequately with the subject. Those involved in sport, however, should gain a better understanding of how they have been injured in the past and how they can prevent further injury in the future.

Basic rules for prevention of sports injuries.

1. FITNESS

Make sure you are fit enough for the sport you are undertaking at the level you are undertaking it. For instance, playing for the first team in any level of football requires a greater level of fitness than to play at a lower grade. This is because the game is usually played at a faster pace and there is a greater degree of physical contact. The majority of sports injuries in field sports take place:

a) In the first few matches of the season - while fitness is building up.

b) In the last quarter of the match - when fatigue sets in.

This can be directly related to the level of fitness of the player.

2. WARMING-UP/WARMING-DOWN.

Sufficient attention to warming-up before any sport is necessary to prevent injuries. It is not uncommon to see a player sprinting for the first time in a game and grabbing the back of his leg in acute pain, with a torn ham-string.

The reasons for warming-up are:

A. TO INCREASE THE BLOOD-FLOW TO THE MUSCLES

B. TO STRETCH THE MUSCLES AND TENDONS

C. THE INCREASED TEMPERATURE OF THE MUSCLE AFTER WARMING UP AND INCREASED FLEXIBILITY AFTER STRETCHING IMPROVES COORDINATION, THEREBY REDUCING THE CHANCE OF INJURY.

D. THE ATHLETE IS MORE RELAXED AND ABLE TO COMPETE AT HIS OPTIMUM LEVEL OF PERFORMANCE.

a. Increased blood-flow.

This is the most important of the three reasons for warming-up.
The working muscle needs fuel. If it doesn't receive sufficient fuel it is much more prone to injury. That fuel is carried by the blood. The body decides how much fuel is needed, by diverting extra blood to the areas that need it. When we are resting, only 10% of the body's blood supply is going to the muscles. However, while exercising this can increase to 75%. This involves opening up blood vessels which are closed unless the muscle is working. Obviously, if there is a delay in reaching that degree of blood-flow, the muscle may be starved of fuel and may be injured.

b. Stretching.

Stretching muscles and tendons is essential to attain maximum performance and to reduce the risk of injury. Stretching particular muscle groups is necessary for different sports, e.g. the big leg muscles - the quadriceps and hamstrings - in runners. This should be done after a general warm-up period to increase the blood-flow.

c. Co-ordination.

The combination of increased blood-flow and stretching improves co-ordination. This makes injury much less likely, whether it is a physical contact sport, in which the body must withstand direct contact, or a technique sport such as javelin-throwing, where the body, or part of it, must withstand an acute strain. The risk of injury can be further reduced by practising a sport-specific movement, such as serving in tennis.

d. Relaxation.

Relaxation, associated with warming-up exercises, defuses excess stress and allows the athlete to perform closer to his optimum level of performance.
The reluctance of certain sportsmen to warm-up is very difficult to understand. It is particularly common in team sports, so coaches must be culpable to a degree. Warming-up should become part of the routine for any individual or team before training for sport and playing sport.

WARMING-UP

Warm-up exercises should be done before both sport and training. In general 10 - 15 minutes should be allowed for warming-up [warming-down involves repeating these exercises for 5 minutes]. You should start with a general warm-up of all the large muscle groups, as described below.

Arms

While standing comfortably, lift your arms up in front of you. When you reach your ears, continue backwards until you have completed the circle. Now do the circle in reverse, starting backwards and bringing your arms the whole way forward. Repeat.

Head and neck

While standing, slowly rotate your head around over your left shoulder; continue to bring it around to the back, allowing it to fall back. Continue over your right shoulder, and allow it to flop gently while rotating it to the front. Repeat.

Shoulders

Shrug your shoulders, hold, and release. Repeat.

Trunk

Stand with your feet apart. Put your hands by your sides. Slowly bring your arm down the side of your leg, without bending forward or bending your knees. Straighten up and repeat down the other side. Repeat.

Legs

Stand with legs apart. Lean forward towards your toes, keeping your back straight. Feel the pull on the back of your legs. Repeat.

Following this you should focus on the part of your body most used in your sport, i.e. the lower limbs in runners. The joints and surrounding structures should be adequately stretched.

When you have completed this, it is a good idea to practice a movement specific to your sport e.g. serving in tennis.

WARMING-DOWN.

Warming-down is a gradual decrease in the exercise you have been doing. It should take place after training and competition. When you finish training or playing suddenly, there is a pooling of blood in the big muscles, as the muscle has stopped pumping the used blood out. This allows a build-up of lactic acid in the muscles - a product of heavy exercise. Cramp results if this is not cleared.

By warming-down you get rid of the blood/lactic acid and let your muscle return to normal. This makes you less prone to injury on exercising again.

Warming-down exercises involve repeating the warming-up exercises for five minutes.

3. THE STRETCHABILITY OF MUSCLES AND TENDONS

This starts decreasing around the age of thirty The affect of this reduction depends on the state of the muscles and tendons at that time, in other words how you have maintained your flexibility and fitness up to that point

Your muscular power decreases at around the same age.

4. EXPERIENCE

With experience you should be able to judge what your body is capable of and also how to avoid getting injured.

5. OBEY THE RULES

The rules are made and adjusted in sport so as to avoid injury.

If a particular activity in sport is responsible for excess injury or serious injury, then the rule-makers of that sport must review the rules governing that activity. An example of this is recent changes in rugby laws regarding the scrum.

If players don't obey the rules of the game, then serious injury may occur.

6. TECHNIQUE

Learning correct technique is crucial in the prevention of injuries. This applies to direct injuries resulting from, for example, poor tackling technique in football or over-use injuries which often result from poor throwing/gripping/running technique. People who have been taught proper technique as children are much less likely to get injured than those who take up games in adulthood, particularly in sports in which there is physical contact.

7. EQUIPMENT

Inadequate equipment, incorrect equipment and not using protective equipment are responsible for a high proportion of preventable sports injuries. In fact, a Canadian survey found that 95% of competitors in contact/ball sports would get an eye injury before the age of 22.if protective equipment was not used. The surveyors showed that correct protective equipment reduced this rate to virtually zero.

We can divide equipment into normal equipment, such as shoes, sports shirts or trousers, and protective equipment which is developed for a specific sport to protect against injury. The division is, however, artificial, as correct normal equipment is protective.

Among the normal equipment, shoes seem to be a major factor. **Wearing shoes which are not designed for the game or surface on which the game is being played, and using damaged footwear is a major problem.** A recent example I have seen is of a referee in gaelic football who wore golf shoes while refereeing a match. He felt he needed extra grip on the hard surface. He developed severe inflammation of both his right and left achilles tendon. After six weeks off sport and after multiple sessions of necessarily painful deep friction from a physiotherapist, he has learned his lesson.

Clothing must be correct for the sport involved. It must be made of the correct materials. For instance, a marathon runner must have a sports vest that will allow ventilation, otherwise he will overheat. Similarly, if the sport involves machinery, the clothes must not be loose enough to catch in the machinery.

Tackling Men's Health

Anybody who has gone horse-riding for a day can tell you why the seats of the jodhpurs are thickened. Chaffing of the thighs can be very painful.

Protective equipment, such as shin pads, riding hats, gum shields, should meet certain specifications:

1. It should not be dangerous to anybody else - .i.e those with whom you come in contact. This obviously applies also to 'normal' equipment also, such as football-boot studs.

2. It must protect, under any foreseeable circumstance, the parts of the body it is protecting. In other words, it must be made of a material which can withstand the pressures likely to be exerted on it. In the case of breakage or distortion - as a result of exceptional strain - it should not be capable of causing major damage itself.

3. It should be easily cleaned. Cleaning must not damage its protective capability.

4. Protective qualities should last a reasonable length of time with obvious signs of wear and tear to signal the need for replacement..

5. It must be designed so as to allow the person wearing it adequate mobility and must not be a source of danger to him.

The design of both sportswear and protective clothing should be subject to strict control and should be under the supervision of a sports medicine committee. At present, fashion, rather than common sense, dictates what is produced.

8. DRUGS.

Your chances of injury are increased considerably by the mis-use of drugs. For instance, excess alcohol consumption the night before competition is associated with an increased incidence of injury. The use of 'performance-enhancing drugs' such as amphetamines is an act of lunacy, as you lose the ability to recognise situations that could lead to your being injured. The effect of amphetamines is to delay the feeling of tiredness in muscles. Muscular performance is not affected. Your judgement of danger, however, is affected.

Death has been the result of this lack of judgement on a few occasions. Anabolic steroids are being abused by those taking part in sports which are strength-orientated, such as weight-lifting, shot-putting and sprinting. They are generally taken by these athletes for four to six weeks in close season. This makes it difficult for the abuse to be detected and explains why testing takes place outside of competition. Anabolic steroids are modified male sex hormones. They increase the muscle bulk. They are associated with both short and long-term-side effects. In the short-term, general effects such as head-ache, nausea and dizziness are common. In addition, the male may experience a reduction in sexual potency. Conversely, the female abuser may also experience an increased sexual potency but may also have an increase in facial hair and deepening of the voice. Long-term use of anabolic steroids can damage beyond repair certain organs in the body, in particular the liver and adrenal glands.

General Treatment of sports injuries:

To treat injuries occurring in sport, you must understand how the injury happened. It is helpful, therefore, to divide sports injuries according to their causes

1. Injuries due to accidents or direct contact.
   a) human contact - kick in the shin
   b) implemental - hit with a racquet
   c) vehicular - fractured collar-bone, e.g., following a fall from a bike

Tackling Men's Health

2. Injuries caused directly by activity.
   a) Incidental - Pulled ham-string achilles tendon
   b) Over-use - these are injuries caused by over-use of a joint or tendon, often related to poor technique or equipment which is not correct for the individual. Examples of this are tennis-elbow or stress-fracture of the leg.

TREATMENT OF OPEN WOUNDS.

Open wounds are those in which the skin is broken. If there is active bleeding:

1. The injured part should be raised. In most cases bleeding can be controlled by raising an arm or a leg.
2. Direct pressure - if you are alone, put pressure directly on the wound. If there is help at hand, apply pressure above and below the wound.
3. Apply a pressure bandage - if the wound is gaping, try to bring the edges together starting below the wound.
   Apply a bandage with some pressure. Continue to apply it until well above the wound. A tourniquet is rarely necessary. If there is no active bleeding the wound should be cleaned. All dirt must be removed. A clean bandage should then be applied. If the wound is deep or gaping, consult your doctor

If infection sets in, see your doctor immediately. You will recognise this if the area becomes red and swollen. It may also feel hot and painful (Heat, redness, pain, swelling)

TETANUS

Protection about infection from tetanus seems to be greatly misunderstood by sportsmen. **Tetanus is a potentially lethal infection**. The tetanus organism produces a poison that attacks nerve transmission. This causes 'lock-jaw', a condition in which the muscles go into spasm as a result of signals from the nerves becoming unclear. If severe, this can cause major problems with breathing, or the person can die of a heart-attack, or of exhaustion due to the frequent muscle spasms.

Infection can occur with any wound no matter how trivial, but is more likely the dirtier and deeper the wound. The organism that causes tetanus is present in high concentration in soil and in faeces. Therefore, anybody playing field sports should be protected.

HOW DO I PROTECT MYSELF?

Protection is achieved by injection of tetanus toxoid under the skin. This produces a reaction in the body which allows it to deal with the nerve poison.if tetanus infects a wound.

TETANUS TOXOID PROTECTION.

1. A single injection provides protection for a short period of time only - 10 weeks approximately
2. Protection is achieved for seven to ten years by three injections given over six months
3. A single booster injection given at the end of seven years provides protection for a further period of seven to ten years. If you do not get a booster at that point you have to start again with a full course of three injections.
4. The childhood injections, 3 in 1 or 2 in 1, which are given as a course of three injections before the age of one contain tetanus toxoid. The pre-school booster injection also contains tetanus toxoid.

Therefore if children have received both their childhood injections and pre-school booster they are immune to tetanus until they are fourteen. If they receive a booster at fourteen, they are covered for another ten years.

Treatment of soft tissue injuries:

The soft tissues are muscles, tendons, ligaments and joints. When these are injured there is bleeding in or around the tissues. The more bleeding that occurs, the more swelling there is.

Swelling has two negative effects.

1. It increases pain because it increases the pressure on the damaged tissues.

2. It slows down healing because the swelling must be cleared out before the body can deal with the injury. Therefore immediate treatment of soft tissue sports injuries is critical to the length of time a sportsman will be out of action. The immediate treatment can be simplified by the RICE method.

R - REST

I - ICE

C - COMPRESSION (ELASTIC BANDAGE)

E - ELEVATION

In addition, there can be early administration of an anti-inflammatory medication, such as aspirin or nurofen, which have been shown to speed recovery rates if administered early. If you have a problem with this form of medication or have a history of stomach problems (e.g. ulcers), then consult your doctor.

R - REST.

This should be self-explanatory but in the heat of competition, the sportsman may continue despite injury. This can lead to a worsening of the injury.

Injury to the leg should be treated by not allowing the person to stand on the injured leg, as weight-bearing may aggravate the injury. The period of rest after the initial 24 hours depends on the severity of the injury.

I - ICE.

This works in two ways. Firstly, it decreases the blood-flow to the affected part, by causing the blood vessels to close up in response to the cold. This reduces the amount of swelling. Secondly, it has an anaesthetic effect on the area itself.

Rules of ice application:
1. NEVER APPLY ICE DIRECTLY ONTO THE SKIN AS THIS CAN CAUSE A COLD BURN. THIS CAN BE PREVENTED BY USING A THIN LAYER OF BANDAGE OR CLOTH.
2. APPLY ICE FOR 10 MINUTES AT A TIME. THE IDEAL TIME FOR PREVENTION OF BLOOD-FLOW IS FOUND TO BE 10 MINUTES. AFTER THIS THE BLOOD VESSELS OPEN UP AGAIN. AFTER REMOVAL, THE ICE CAN BE RE-APPLIED IN A SHORT PERIOD OF TIME.

Ice can be bought at sports events, either as disposable ice packs or re-usable ice packs. The disposable pack contains two chemicals which are brought into contact by a hard squeeze on the pack. When they meet they cause a cold reaction. The main disadvantage of these packs is cost. The re-usable packs are made of a gel which is frozen in a refrigerator before use. If it is brought to a sports event it must be kept in a cooling bag until needed.

C - COMPRESSION.

An elasticated bandage applied after the injury limits the space available for swelling, which helps the body to stop the bleeding itself. The bandage can be applied with ice underneath it (one layer of bandage protecting the skin). It should be applied starting at the bottom end, i.e. nearer the toes, if the injury is in the leg. The bandage should extend well above and below the injury. If the athlete complains of severe pain or pins and needles below the bandage, or if the skin of the toes or fingers have poor circulation, then the bandage should be removed as it is causing problems with blood getting to the extremities.

E - ELEVATION.

By elevating the injury, swelling is reduced in two ways. Firstly, less blood is pumped into the area as it has to go uphill. Secondly, the drainage of the swelling is easier as it is going downhill. The more it is elevated the better - within the limits of comfort. Pressure should be kept off the back of the calf while elevating the leg for prolonged periods, as blockage of drainage from the calf can lead to clot formation. If using cushions, place them under the heel rather than the calf.

Depending on the severity of the injury, medical advice should be sought. If, initially, the injury is thought not to be severe enough for a medical opinion but if there is ongoing severe pain or if you are unsure as to what is wrong, then a medical opinion should be sought.

If there has been a dislocation of any joint, such as a finger or shoulder, which has already been put back in place by a doctor or someone else at the scene, the injured part should still be seen by a doctor and x-rayed. This is necessary for two reasons.

Firstly, there may be an associated fracture (break) around the joint. Secondly, correct strapping of the joint makes recurrence much less likely. This is because strapping limits movement and allows the ligaments and muscles, which keep the joint stable, to heal.

Further treatment of soft tissue injuries:

This depends on their severity. The principles of treatment are:

>R<small>EPAIR</small>
>R<small>EST</small>
>R<small>EHABILITATION</small>

REPAIR.

Repair of soft tissue may take place naturally in the case of minor soft tissue injuries. However, moderate or severe injuries require help. This help may be from the athlete's own doctor, the physiotherapist, or occasionally the surgeon.

MUSCLE INJURIES.

These can be caused by over-loading, e.g. a pulled hamstring in a sprinter, or by direct contact, e.g. 'dead leg' in a footballer.

The over-load injury is usually more difficult to treat. When the muscles tear there is bleeding into the deeper part of the muscle itself. [With the direct contact injury the bleeding is more superficial.] The blood forms a clot which occupies the space left as the muscles retract with injury. Treatment is aimed at getting the blood-clot to break up so as to allow both ends of the muscle to meet. This allows better healing to take place. The break-up of the blood-clot can be helped considerably by physiotherapy with a chartered physiotherapist. The techniques available to speed up the process include ice, heat, electrical stimulation, ultra-sound and deep friction or massage. In the direct contact injury, the bleeding is outside the muscle, within the muscle sheath. After initial treatment as described, they usually settle reasonably rapidly. This process can be stepped up by the physiotherapist.

Occasionally, complete rupture may occur. This may require surgical repair. At surgery, the clot can be removed and the two muscles brought together. Theoretically, this should lead to very good results but in general the results of surgical repair are not as good as one would have expected. This is mainly due to the prolonged period of rest necessary for healing to take place. This delays early rehabilitation of the injured part.

TENDON INJURIES

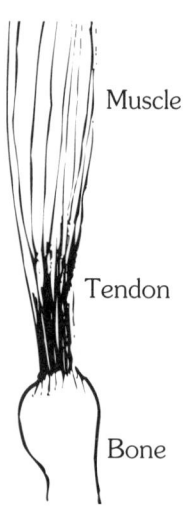

Tendons are the strong structures by which the muscles are attached to the bone. They are able to withstand the strain produced by a very strong pull of the muscle. The tendon can be injured, either by rupturing (tearing) or by becoming inflamed (tendinitis). Rupture can vary from slight tear to complete tear,. and becomes more common with age due to the reduced elasticity of the tendon and to the possibility of previous damage to the tendon. Rupture of the achilles tendon has been found to take place at a site of degeneration (break-down) of the fibres of the tendon. This usually occurs at a part of the tendon where the blood supply is limited.

The treatment of complete tendon rupture is usually surgical repair followed by a period of 6-12 weeks in plaster of paris. The correct early treatment of partial tears of the tendon is of critical importance to the sportsman as untreated, or inadequately treated, they become chronic problems and even lead to early retirement. Treatment involves the injured tendon being immobilised and rested for a lengthy period. The physiotherapist may be able to help in speeding up the healing process with, for instance, ultra-sound and friction. In addition, the tendon fibres heal in better alignment after friction.

Inflammation of the tendon occurs where there has been an increase in activity or training-load. Rest and deep friction by a physiotherapist are the most effective treatments. Local injection with steroids may be considered by your doctor, if appropriate (never around the Achilles tendon as rupture of the Achilles tendon may result)

LIGAMENT INJURIES

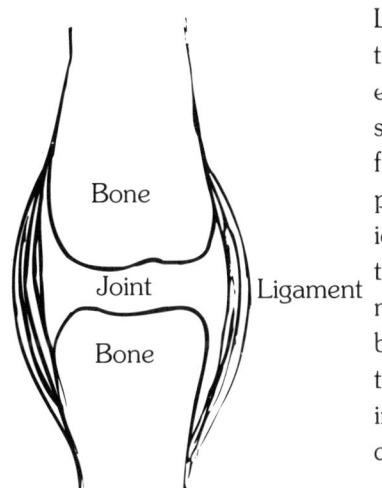

Ligaments are the tissues that help to maintain the stability of the joints of the body. They generally span the area of the joint where the strain is likely to be greatest. When excessive force is applied to the ligament, it can either partially or fully tear. The ankle sprain is a typical example of this. After initial emergency treatment (R.I.C.E.) to the injury, the joint must be tested for stability. If the joint is unstable, further investigation - i.e. special x-rays of the ankle or arthroscopy of the knees (looking into the knee joint with a scope), may be required.

If the joint is stable, then treatment will involve strapping or taping. Early exercise of the affected joint and surrounding muscles will follow soon afterwards, for instance walking with crutches after knee or ankle injury. This is particularly important in weight-bearing joints, as they lose their balance perception and become more prone to future injury. A physiotherapist speeds recovery and ensures that the sportsman does not resume his sport until fit to do so.

REST.

This period of rest needed for a sports injury depends on the type of tissue injured and the severity of that injury. Rest involves only the injured part and the rest of the body can be kept in shape, even when resting the injury. Rest can be from exercises which stretch the muscle, but may allow exercises where the muscle is put into action without affecting the length of the muscle, for instance holding a weight in your hand with the arm stretched out.

REHABILITATION.

This starts as early as possible after the injury, even before the pain is fully gone. It involves maintaining the movement of the joint and ligaments, and the stretch and flexibility of the muscles and tendons. Rehabilitation continues even after the player has resumed his sport, as the injured part may require strapping.

Over-use Injuries

The vast majority of over-use injuries occur in two types of sportsman.

    1. Endurance athletes - marathon runners etc.

As the stress associated with this activity is taken on the lower-limb, these injuries are almost exclusively of the lower-limb. 90% of the increased stress is absorbed by the soft tissues of the lower-limb. The tibia takes most of the rest of the stress. The soft tissues and tibia are therefore the structures at greatest risk of injury.

    2. Sportsmen involved in repetitive skilled movements, usually one-man sports, such as racquet sports or weight-lifting.

Repeated minor microscopic injury seems to be the major cause of over-use injury. The initial minor injury may not produce any symptoms, but continuing to play brings about further minor injury. The athlete is eventually forced to stop running/playing.

The endurance athlete, as noted above, usually suffers his injury in the legs. Stress-fracture occurs where a repetitive load is put on the leg. It may occur in one leg due to a fault in the structure of that leg, e.g. flat feet, an imbalance in the muscles of the leg, poor equipment, e.g. shoes, or due to the surface on which the athlete is running, e.g. running a training course with slopes that put all the strain on one leg. The strain causes a minuscule break in the bone. This may not cause pain while resting but when the athlete attempts to exercise, pain develops. Initially, it may take running a long distance for pain to develop but gradually, as the repeated stress on the leg causes the fracture to extend, the athlete becomes unable to exercise without pain. Even at this stage x-ray may not show the fracture and a special scan may be necessary.

TENNIS ELBOW.

The act of hitting a tennis ball involves the racquet to be gripped correctly, the racquet and arm absorbing the impact of the ball on the racquet, and the imparting of force onto the ball to get it across the net. How the body deals with this repeatedly depends on a combination of muscle balance, co-ordination, technique, equipment and the surface on which you are playing. The force of all of this is taken by the muscle that cocks up your wrists (extends). This muscle's tendon is attached to bone at the outer part of the elbow. If there is a fault in any of these factors listed above, an excessive force is transmitted to the point where the tendon comes off the bone. This causes a small area of damage. However, before that area has a chance to heal, the tendon is stretched again. This sets up a vicious circle of attempted healing followed by re-injury. There is increasing inflammation which causes increasing pain. Treatment of the injury must therefore involve not only stopping the inflammation, but an appraisal of the patient's arm, his racquet, and his technique. (For treatment see Elbow injuries later in this chapter).

Over-use injuries occur in competitive top-level athletes in their twenties and in non-competitive athletes in their thirties. This can be explained by the severe strains put on the athlete during his high-intensity training and performance in his twenties. Any fault in technique, muscle-balance or any body fault will have come to light by the time the athlete reaches his thirties. The non-competitive athlete becomes injured at a time of decreasing elasticity in his tendons. This means their ability to withstand pressure is less.

The treatment of fractures is outside the scope of this chapter. Suffice to say that fracture treatment involves the injured part being immobilised, by a sling, plaster of paris, or various forms of metal pins or screws. Rehabilitation is therefore of crucial importance. The non-injured parts must be kept alive by exercise but some activity of the injured limb can usually be started when the patient is still immobilised.

Treatment of head, neck, eye, ear, chest and abdomen injuries are beyond the scope of this chapter, except for the basic rules below.

HEAD INJURY

A doctor's opinion should be sought and the sportsman should stop playing if there is subsequently:
1. LOSS OF CONSCIOUSNESS - EVEN IF THIS HAS ONLY LASTED A FEW SECONDS
2. A PERSISTENT HEADACHE
3. PERSISTENT NAUSEA, VOMITING OR DIZZINESS
4. DOUBLE-VISION
5. BREATHING DIFFICULTIES, NECK INJURIES

The athlete should not be moved without expert advice if he is complaining of:
1. SEVERE NECK PAIN AFTER IMPACT OR SCRUM COLLAPSE
2. PAIN RADIATING FROM HIS NECK DOWN HIS ARM

3. PINS AND NEEDLES DOWN HIS ARM
4. LOSS OF POWER IN ANY OF HIS LIMBS, EVEN TRANSIENT LOSS OF POWER
5. BREATHING DIFFICULTIES AFTER NECK INJURY

IF THE ATHLETE DEVELOPS NECK PAIN AFTER SPORT HE SHOULD SEEK MEDICAL ADVICE.

EYE INJURIES

These can be caused by the ball, racquet, or by opposing players. People with eye-sight problems should be careful to use spectacles or contact lenses that are suitable for the sport they are playing. If the eye receives a direct injury involving loss of vision, then medical advice should be urgently sought. Early treatment of serious eye injuries is of paramount importance.

EAR INJURIES

Where there is loss of hearing and/or bleeding from the ear-hole, ear injuries require medical assessment as there may be perforation of the eardrum.

CHEST INJURIES

As the chest contains the heart and the lungs, chest injuries are potentially serious. Any breathing difficulties after a chest injury should alert the athlete to seek help.

ABDOMINAL INJURIES

Medical attention should be sought if there is
1 PERSISTENT ABDOMINAL PAIN
2 BLEEDING FROM ANY SOURCE, E.G. BLOOD IN THE URINE, VOMITING OF BLOOD;

SCROTAL INJURIES

These usually occur as a result of direct contact. If there is considerable pain and/or swelling, then medical attention should be sought as a matter of some urgency.

Common Sports Injuries:

This is not a comprehensive coverage of sports injuries, but rather a personal selection of the soft tissue injuries seen in general practice or sports injury clinics. I have excluded fractures and dislocations in this instance.

UPPER-ARM INJURIES

SHOULDER INJURIES.

Injuries of the shoulder usually give pain at a spot a third of the way between the shoulder and the elbow - no matter what the cause. This creates difficulties with some sportsmen as they wonder why the doctor/physiotherapist is not treating them directly at that spot.

The painful arc.

If your arm is lifted out to the side and initially there is no pain, then as it is raised further your shoulder becomes painful [usually between 70%-120%], and then as your arm is brought up towards your ear the pain goes, you have a painful arc. The painful arc occurs if an inflamed tissue is being caught between the bones as the shoulder is raised [see diagram].

Causes of the painful arc:
1. Tendinitis
2. Bursitis

1. Tendinitis

Inflammation of a tendon
- one of three tendons or occasionally two of the three tendons may be injured.

a) Supraspinatus Tendinitis - the commonest form of painful arc
b) Infraspinatus Tendinitis.
c) Subscapular Tendinitis

a) Supraspinatus Tendinitis

This is an over-use injury. The supraspinatus muscle is responsible for firstly bringing the arm out to the side and also for turning the shoulder outward. Therefore an activity such as serving in tennis, where the arm is repeatedly held above shoulder level, can lead to tendinitis.

Treatment Options:

1. Medication and rest - anti-inflammation medication and rest from the activity which is causing pain may be successful in very early cases.

2. Physiotherapy - the physiotherapist may use various treatments, but the most successful appears to be deep friction, where the physio isolates the inflamed tendon and deeply massages it.

3. Steroid injection - injection of steroid stops the inflammation of the tendon and allows it time to heal. Following the injection, rest is mandatory for two weeks as the tendon may snap if excessively strained during this period.

4. Surgery - Surgery may be necessary where the condition has become chronic or where the tendon has ruptured.

b + c)

Treatment of the less common infraspinatus tendinitis and subscapular tendinitis is based on similar techniques but is aimed specifically at the injured tendons.

2. Bursitis

The body has small fluid-filled sacs which occupy spaces around joints where there are moving parts in contact. These are called Bursae. The bursa in the shoulder lies over the tendons and stops the tendons getting worn down by the bone above. This fluid-filled sac can become inflamed.

Subacromial bursitis;

This can be caused by a fall or by repetitive movements.

Treatment options:

1. Aspiration - that is taking fluid out of the bursa through a needle. This is particularly important if the injury follows a fall or direct contact, as the bursa probably contains blood. Failure to remove the blood may allow the condition to become chronic.

2. Rest and anti-inflammation tablets.

3.

a) Injection of local anaesthetic. This is useful in the early stages of bursitis and appears to allow the injury to settle.

b) injection of steroid. This is useful where the condition has become chronic.

4. Surgery - removal of the bursa may be necessary in resistant cases.

Elbow Injuries

The common soft tissue injuries around the elbow are:
1. TENNIS ELBOW
2. GOLFER'S ELBOW
3. THROWER'S ELBOW
4. JAVELIN-THROWER'S ELBOW
5. BASEBALL ELBOW

TENNIS ELBOW

The way this develops is described in detail under over-use injuries [see page ...]. Pain at the outside of the elbow is the main feature, usually made worse by gripping anything tightly.

Treatment of tennis elbow
1. Rest and anti-inflammation medication - early cases.
2. Physiotherapy - Treatment usually involves deep friction to the area of injury, after it has been partially anaesthetised by ice application. Following successful treatment, the physio will begin an exercise programme aimed at preventing recurrences
3. Injection of steroid locally - steroid injection into the tender spot. This can initially increase the pain. Rest for ten days after the injection is necessary. The injection may need to be repeated at that time.
4. Manipulation - this acts by opening out the painful scar, breaking the circle of recurrent inflammation and allowing the tendon to heal
5. Surgery - in persistent cases, cutting the affected tendon at operation may be necessary. The results of the operation are generally good.

To reduce the likelihood of recurrence of tennis elbow:

1. Review weight of racquet
2. Review size of grip
3. Review technique - get professional coaching if necessary
4. Stop playing tennis in the rain, wet tennis balls are heavier and add to the friction
5. Use tight forearm strapping below the elbow

GOLFER'S ELBOW:

This condition occurs on the inner side of the elbow. It is much less common and is much less disabling that tennis elbow. The tendon affected is the tendon of the muscle that bends the wrist down, the flexor muscle. It is not confined to golfers as tennis players may develop it, with the serving action. In right-handed golfers it arises in the right elbow [tennis elbow occurs in the left elbow of right-handed golfers], as a result of taking too large a divot while chipping.

Treatment

Treatment options are the same as for tennis elbow, except that the manipulation of golfer's elbow is not usually used, as it is not as successful as the manipulation for tennis elbow.

FOREARM INJURIES

The major problem in this area is inflammation of the sheath covering the tendons of the forearm. It is called Tenosynovitis and occurs particularly in rowers or canoeists early in their season. When this condition is severe, there is swelling of the forearm which, when pressed, gives the same sensation as touching crepe paper [Crepitus is the medical term for this]

Treatment:
1. Rest - Rest from sport until symptoms settle; strapping, or plaster of paris for a week or longer
2. Injection - an injection of steroid into the sheath followed by rest.

CARPAL TUNNEL SYNDROME

At the wrist, the tendons on the palm side are kept in place by a tight band. This forms a tunnel between the tendons. The nerve which gives sensation to the thumb and the two fingers beside it runs through this tunnel. If swelling develops in this tunnel, then pain and/or pins and needles will develop in these fingers. This can arise in sportsmen as a result of;

1. Racquet sports - repeated wrist movements
2. Tenosynovitis - the swelling associated with the inflammation of the tendon sheath.
3. After fracture of the wrist
4. Hand infection

It can also arise as a result of certain general medical conditions such as thyroid gland problems.

Treatment
1. Rest and anti-inflammation medication - rest from a repetitive action may be necessary.
2. "Cock-Up" splint - a night-time splint with the wrist cocked-up can give good relief from night-time symptoms.
3. Injection of steroid - an injection of steroid under the band into the tunnel can reduce swelling.
4. Surgery - at operation the band is divided. This is generally successful.

LOWER LIMB INJURIES:

GROIN STRAIN - 'RIDER'S STRAIN'

This common injury arises when one of the muscles that draw the leg inwards is over-loaded. This causes part of the tendon of the muscle to pull off the pelvis in the groin. There may be pain initially which settles after the game/training is finished. However, when the athlete resumes, he gets the pain back worse than ever.

Treatment options:

Seek treatment in the early stages - this is a very difficult condition if it becomes chronic.
1. Rest and anti-inflammation tablets. In my experience, this is rarely successful with this condition.
2. Physiotherapy - deep friction and other forms of treatment.
3. Injection of steroid - this is usually only successful if the tenderness is specific at the junction of bone and tendon.
4. Surgery

A rehabilitation programme is essential after treatment of this injury.

'PULLED' HAMSTRING

A pulled hamstring is a partial rupture of the hamstring muscle. The sprinter grabbing the back of his thigh, thirty yards into the sprint, demonstrates pulling a hamstring perfectly. The early treatment of this injury with R.I.C.E. is crucial as the tear is often deep in this bulky muscle. Without early treatment there is therefore a big clot deep down in this bulk. It is very hard for the physiotherapist to get his/her hands working effectively through the bulk to speed up healing and reduce the clot, thereby reducing the amount of scarring of the muscle. It is the extent of the scarring with this injury that allows it to recur with such frequency.

Treatment

1. R.I.C.E (see earlier in this chapter).
2. Physiotherapy:
- Ice/heat
- treatment with electrical equipment
- deep friction
- maintain muscle and joint movement
- assess the way the leg works to see if there is a correctable fault in the structure or working of the leg.
- follow the sportsman's progress with a gradual exercise programme until he is fully rehabilitated, i.e. has returned to full activity at his level in sport.
3. Surgery may occasionally be necessary.

THE KNEE:

The knee is one of the most frequently injured joints in sport, particularly in contact sport. In most sports, a stable knee joint is necessary for the sportsman to be able to continue to play. The knee is kept stable firstly by the big muscles that surround it and secondly, by a ligament on each side of the joint [collateral ligaments], two ligaments inside the joint [cruciate ligaments], and by two shock-absorbers within the joint [the cartilage or meniscus]. When the lower leg is hit with force from, for example, the outer side, the structures on the inner side of the knee are all put under strain.

Therefore, depending on the force and angle of injury, the following injuries could occur:

1. Partial or full tear of the ligament at the inner side of the knee [medial collateral ligament].
2. Tear of the cartilage on the inner part of the joint [medial meniscus tear].
3. Tear of one of the ligaments inside the joint [anterior cruciate ligament].
4. Tear of the second ligament inside the knee [posterior cruciate].

As can be seen from this, knee injuries are complicated and should receive expert attention. This is particularly true where, following injury, swelling of the knee joint takes place very quickly i.e., in the first hour, as this suggests structures inside the joint have been damaged. Early orthopaedic assessment and arthroscopy are essential. Arthroscopy involves looking into the joint with a small scope. Any blood can be sucked out and the extent of the internal damage assessed.

Treatment of the ligaments outside the knee follows the guidelines on ligament injuries outlined earlier in this chapter.

SPRAINED ANKLE

The commonest of all sports injuries. Classically, it involves the foot being pushed inwards with undue strain on the outer (lateral) ligaments of the ankle. In most cases this causes a tear of one of the ligaments. However, if the strain is greater, further ligaments may be torn and tendons over-stretched. Proper treatment of sprained ankle is essential as, improperly treated, two major problems can develop: